The Information Game

Studies in Applied Philosophy
Series Editors: Brenda Almond and Anthony O'Hear

Published

Igor Primoratz
Justifying Legal Punishment

Geoffrey Brown
The Information Game:
Ethical Issues in a Microchip World

The Information Game

Ethical Issues in a Microchip World

Geoffrey Brown

Humanities Press International, Inc.
New Jersey ◇ London

First published in 1990 in the United States of America by
Humanities Press International, Inc.,
Atlantic Highlands, NJ 07716 and
3 Henrietta Street, London WC2E 8LU

©Geoffrey Brown, 1990

Library of Congress Cataloging-in-Publication Data

Brown, Geoffrey, 1953–
    The Information game: ethical issues in a microchip world /
Geoffrey Brown.
        p. cm. — (Studies in applied philosophy)
    Bibliography: p.
    Includes index.
    ISBN 0–391–03575–4
    1. Information technology—Moral and ethical aspects. 2. Data
bases—Moral and ethical aspects. 3. Computers—Access control—
Moral and ethical aspects. 4. Privacy, Right of. I. Title.
II. Series: Studies in applied philosophy (Atlantic Highlands, N.J.)
HC79, 155B76 1990
174'.9092—dc19   88—8289
                                                            CIP

British Cataloging in Publication Data

A CIP record for this book is available from the British Library.

Printed in the United States of America

Contents

AUTHOR'S PREFACE   vi

INTRODUCTION   vii

1	New Problems for Old	1
2	Technology as Morally Neutral	21
3	Is Big Brother Watching?	37
4	To Err Is Human	57
5	Private Lives	67
6	More about Privacy	81
7	The Non-Human Face of Technology	95
8	Ownership, Rights, and Information	105
9	Moral Attitudes to Machines?	121
10	The Variety of Remedies	135

Notes   153

Bibliography   157

Index   161

Author's Preface

With great pleasure I would like to acknowledge the kindness of the Institute of Philosophy, of the Catholic University of Leuven (Belgium), in offering me the visiting professorship during which this book was largely written.

Among the many individuals for whose help and encouragement I am grateful are Brenda Almond, Mike Bavidge, William Charlton, Martin Hughes, Geoffrey and Mary Midgley, and all the staff and students of the Philosophy Department in the University of Newcastle upon Tyne, England.

I would also like to thank Anthony O'Hear, whose idea it originally was that I should write this book. Special thanks are due to my wife Valerie, who assisted with the research. All mistakes and other shortcomings are, needless to say, entirely my own.

Newcastle upon Tyne

Introduction

Asked what feature of our environment has done most to change life in developed countries in the past couple of decades, most people would probably say, after not much hesitation, "computers." By this they would probably mean any or all of a number of things, from micros to distributed networks, from electronic games to data banks, which are often meant to be covered by this blanket term. When actually asked in a survey in the United States, 86 percent of respondents believed that life had changed significantly as a result of computerization, though 71 percent thought it had changed for the better and 15 percent that it had changed for the worse! As many as 34 percent, however, reported that they had experienced problems as a result of computers.[1]

It is inconceivable that any development which has changed the face of everyday life as much as information technology should not have far-reaching ethical consequences. It is these consequences with which we shall be concerned in this book. Perhaps the most obvious relate to the ease with which information on individuals can be stored, processed, and retrieved using computers. It is by now a commonplace to say that we live in a society in which it is possible to acquire, retain, and retrieve information, including personal information about individuals, far more easily and efficiently than ever in the past. This has brought many undeniable benefits. More information can be made available to the public more readily, and the opportunity for democratic decision-making is thereby enhanced. It is now more convenient than formerly to order goods, pay bills, keep accounts, and so on. Innumerable aspects of life have become less tedious as a result of our new electronic environment.

However, as indicated by the above survey, not everyone is satisfied that the results of the ongoing "technological revolution" are proving uniformly beneficial. Data banks containing diverse information about individuals have become objects of suspicion and even of hostility, and the need has been widely recognized for some legal control of data storage.[2] Not only are particular pieces of information on persons more easily available to a greater number of agencies, but also the possibility for combining and assembling such data has been thought to raise special problems concerning liberty, personal privacy, and other aspects of the ethics of public life. Furthermore, once information has been gathered and stored in such a way, it is liable to remain on file long after it is needed, and thereby to outlive its accuracy as well as its proper usefulness — if, that is, it was accurate in the first place, which some people think less likely the more of the task is left to a machine. These are only a very few of the ways in which the world of electronically encoded facts is thought by many to be a dangerous and uncongenial one to the individual. They are at the root of some of the chief ethical issues which I have chosen to discuss in this book.

The task of doing so has both encouraging and discouraging sides to it. The broad sweep which is necessary to encompass the problems involved is both exhilarating and daunting. Moreover, it is a subject about which traditional moral philosophy has little to say. As a result one is to some extent spared the necessity of looking continually over one's shoulder, or of digesting the small library of existing literature which tends to confront those pursuing more well-worn philosophical tracks. On the other hand, however, the philosopher who embarks on such an enterprise is to that extent deprived of any clear guidelines, the pitfalls are still unmarked, and one must make one's own mistakes and false starts.

It may well be asked why it should be thought the business of the philosopher to delve into such issues as information technology. Despite the rapid growth of what is sometimes called applied philosophy, there is a certain amount of skepticism rife regarding the propriety of philosophers venturing beyond the bounds of purely conceptual study and talking about something which is specific to a particular period and requires some specialist knowledge of a particular subject area. I hope that the answer to this question will come out in the ensuing discussion, for this book is partly an attempt to answer that question by showing what can be done in this way — whether successful or not is another matter.

One thing which I hope will emerge, and which lends much support to the view that philosophers have a role to play in clarifying and deliberating on "real life" problems, is how quickly these specific and localized problems open up into much broader conceptual ones once the surface of them is scratched. Too often when this happens, the first reaction of the policy-makers is to sweep the conceptual question under the carpet or to answer it summarily by appealing to mere prejudice or common sense (which often amounts to the same thing, and tends to break down easily where the problems concerned are unfamiliar ones).

Chapter 1 is an overview of the ways in which information technology presents problems of a moral character. In chapter 2 I move on to consider the relations between technology and ethics regarding the moral neutrality, or otherwise, of inventions and discoveries. Chapter 3 introduces the first specific issue, which concerns the potential role of information technology in political oppression and the establishment of an Orwellian totalitarian state. In chapter 4 I leave behind the issue of deliberate harm caused via such technology and look at the question of accidental harm caused by the (supposedly notorious) "errors" of machines. Chapters 5 and 6 deal with the important concept of privacy and the effects of data technology on the privacy of individuals' lives. In chapter 7 I consider the vaguer, but no less significant and forceful, idea that computerization has had the effect of dehumanizing our existence, and the question of how, if at all, this process could be halted or reversed. Chapter 8 tackles ethical issues of ownership and property raised by computer technology. The last specific issue, which will be considered briefly in chapter 9, is the more exotic question of whether we may someday be led to take a moral stance toward computers themselves. Finally, chapter 10 presents some suggested remedies for the problems and dilemmas raised earlier in the book.

A couple of points of terminology ought to be made clear at this point. First, for the benefit of those unfamiliar with moral philosophy, the words "ethical" and "moral" are generally speaking used interchangeably, and this practice will be adopted here. Secondly, I have already used the expressions "computer," "computer technology," "information technology," "machines," "networks," and "data banks." Some of these will be explained later in the text, but where no explanation of such terms and the distinctions between them is offered, it can safely be assumed that the explanation is not necessary to our purposes.

One thing, however, which this whole family of terms has in common, is that they are all to do with information, with its storage, manipulation, and retrieval. It is, then, the ethical, or moral, aspects of information technology, taken in a fairly general sense, which will form the theme of this book. Lastly, it might be asked: Why the suggestion in the title that information technology is in some sense a "game"? Is this meant to imply that it is unimportant, frivolous, or peripheral to the real issues of life? The explanation, I am afraid, will have to wait until the last chapter.

1. New Problems for Old

And the anger of the Lord was kindled against Israel, and he moved David against them to say, Go, number Israel and Judah. For the king said to Joab the captain of the host, which was with him, Go now through all the tribes of Israel, from Dan even to Beer-sheba, and number ye the people, that I may know the number of the people.... And Joab gave up the sum of the number of the people unto the king: and there were in Israel eight hundred thousand valiant men that drew the sword; and the men of Judah were five hundred thousand men. And David's heart smote him after that he had numbered the people. And David said unto the Lord, I have sinned greatly in that I have done: and now, I beseech thee, O Lord, take away the iniquity of thy servant; for I have done very foolishly.

II Samuel 24

The ethics of information, its gathering, possession, and use, is not altogether a new topic. Maybe we shall never know the exact nature of the theological objection to census-taking in ancient Israel. Nevertheless, we are all more or less familiar with various contemporary worries concerning the nature and extent of the records which are, or might be, kept on each one of us. Some of these records will be in the possession of what, for the time being, we may loosely call officialdom. Others will be in the files of private companies and other agencies.

But in recent times, and particularly within the last couple of decades, a new factor has entered. This is the advent of what might be called the large-scale use of small-scale technology. In other words, the widespread use of devices capable of storing data in a minute form, and therefore of storing much more of it. We call these beasts computers, though this is perhaps something of a misnomer, for only a small proportion of what they actually do can properly be called computation. To a large extent they may be compared to miniscule electronic card-indexes with astonishing capacities, not just for storage of data but for its retrieval and analysis. So great is the difference between this kind of technology and what people have been used to in the way of record-keeping in the past, that the difference of degree might be said to amount to a difference in kind. Correspondingly, the ethics connected with the use of such technology has sometimes been said to present us with a new moral problem, or set of moral problems. Before going on to talk about the kinds of problems presented, I would like to discuss the very idea of a moral problem being a novel one.

A New Moral Problem?

Under what circumstances are we entitled to claim that we are dealing with a "new" moral problem? One, that is, which is not just a new form of an old one, nor simply one which is unfamiliar to a particular agent, but one which is of a type that has never before arisen for the moral community of which we are a part? It is wise not to be too rash in claiming such novelty, though cases like this do sometimes arise.

One way in which this might happen is through a discovery or scientific development which upsets the moral categories with which we are used to dealing. This could happen if we became able to perform brain transplant operations, or perhaps if we were to discover humanoid beings on another planet and were not sure whether to treat them as moral agents or not. A similar problem (touched on in chapter 9) concerns the possibility that machines might some day attain a level of complexity and sophistication which would make it appropriate to take a moral stance toward them. To an extent, the question of the moral status of non-human animals is, insofar as it has only recently been widely recognized, new in this way. The same may be said of some issues arising out of recent advances affecting human reproduction (sperm banks, surrogate motherhood, and the like).

Another sense in which a moral problem might have a novel aspect is that it might lead people to talk about the need to "create new values," a phrase often heard in certain schools of moral philosophy. I do not intend to go into the thorny issues involved here (which would open up for us the entire dispute between ethical "naturalists" and "non-naturalists"), except to say that I do not believe any problem or situation could require us to invent new values, for the simple reason that it cannot be done. Despite such writers as Nietzsche[1] and, more recently, B.F. Skinner,[2] the idea of such invention is simply incoherent. For if we have a reason for intro-ducing new values, they cannot be genuinely new, since the values which are really being implemented are the ones embodied in the reason which we have for it. If, on the other hand, we do not have a reason, then, *ex hypothesi*, we have no reason. If our values really are values, that is, fundamental goods as opposed to the norms which we adopt in pursuit of those goods, there can be nothing further in the light of which it might become appropriate to alter them. We do, of course, often have to balance one value or set of values against another. We also discover values, such as that of individual freedom, for example, in the course of human development. But neither of these things is the same thing as being confronted with a problem which dictates the need for new basic values. This hardly adds up to a full argument, but is rather a sketch of what such an argument would be like if there were the space or the necessity to pursue it here.

There is yet a third sense in which every moral problem might be said to be a new one. The circumstances are never precisely the same in two different cases, and much has been made of this by existentialists and by the proponents of situation ethics. This presents certain difficulties, chiefly about the alleged universalizability of moral principles, but this need not worry us unduly here. Everyone knows that there are enough relevant similarities between cases to make some ethical principles and generalizations possible.

The kind of ethical problem posed by the advent of new data technology does not fit neatly into any of these categories. Despite what I have already said about its staggering effect on our capacity for record-keeping, and despite all that has been written on the way in which computer technology is set to change our lives beyond recognition, it does not seem that any real conceptual shift or reorganization of our moral categories is indicated. Not only "new" moral problems are new in this very strong sense or require such spectacular readjustment. Indeed, one trouble with them is that they often arise so gradually and inconspicuously that we do not notice them until it is too late — that is, until inadequate, unjust, or ill-conceived "solutions" already hold the field by default. Nor can it be a case of needing to rethink our fundamental moral values. It is, however, possible to see why people should think this. For the reality is that we are sometimes required to respond to altered circumstances in ways which involve new ways of respecting existing values. For example, the practice of contraception was once widely attacked by appealing to the value or sanctity of human life. In a world aware of the dangers of overpopulation and food shortages, it is now advocated by appeal to just that same basic value. In something like this way I would prefer to view the problems set before us by advanced information technology. Not as a single cataclysmic shock to our culture which should panic us into an heroic attempt at rethinking our moral attitudes in this area from scratch; but rather as a set of "middle range" moral problems needing careful and calm consideration. In later chapters I have divided these problems up for separate treatment, but in the remainder of this chapter I would like to say something about what many of them have in common, and how they originate.

The Shifting Pattern of Information

It is now time for a little crude and homespun sociology, which I think is not misleading and is necessary for what follows. One can identify a traditional pattern, common to nearly all periods and societies, in which for any typical individual (that is, not a public figure or celebrity) a large number of people will know a little about him or her, and a few people will know a great deal. That recent developments in information-gathering represent a movement away from this kind of pattern is fairly obvious. The traditional pattern might be characterized as being such that:

(a) Those relationships which involve access by one person to extensive information regarding another would normally be open to control by the individuals in question.
(b) Accordingly, the identity of the person who had such access would be known to the subject of the information.
(c) The relationship would usually be reciprocal: if, for example, one's neighbors knew everything of significance about oneself (age, ancestry, personal history, financial status, and so forth) one would also have access to the same sorts of information concerning them, thus lending the situation a kind of equilibrium.
(d) The nature of the information possessed by others would be known to the subject (although one might not know exactly what information was in circulation regarding oneself, one would at least have a good idea of its general character).

The significance of (a) will be discussed at some length later in the book, but here I want to say a little about (b), (c), and (d). These may be jointly summed up by saying that access to such information in what I have termed the traditional pattern would be a matter of what might be called "common knowledge." Common knowledge can exist between members of any group of a size small enough to give rise to the requisite conditions. Taking a group of just two persons as a paradigm, we may say that a piece of knowledge is common knowledge if it is the case that A knows it and B knows it, and A knows that B knows it, and B knows that A knows it, and A knows that B knows that A knows it . . . and so on. The extent of the "and so on" is a problem with which I shall make no attempt to deal here — it is likely that at some not-clearly-defined point the addition of further clauses simply ceases to contribute anything significant.[3] Now, where the information involved is not just a single item of knowledge but a whole category of information, we may say analogously that a category of information is common between two persons when A has access to it and B has access to it, and A knows that B has access to it, and B knows that A has access to it, and A knows that B knows that A has access to it . . . and so on. And where the group is conceived of as a group of any arbitrary size, and where one category of information which is common is that which concerns personal information about the individuals themselves, we have a description of this aspect of what I called the traditional pattern. Its essence may be summed up by the word "reciprocity." Given such a pattern, extensive personal information about someone, if it is accessible at all, will be accessible as a result of its belonging to a category of information which is common within some group of which both the knower and the subject of the information are members.

The trend away from such a pattern did not begin with the invention of the computer, or even of the filing cabinet. It may plausibly be thought to have begun with the movement of populations from rural to urban environments, which has occurred at different times in different parts of the world, and the resulting growth of towns and cities, which created a greater degree of anonymity and a greater separation of the masses from the locus of the officialdom to which they are immediately responsible. It is clear, however, that the trend away from this traditional kind of pattern has been given enormously greater momentum by the methods which now exist for surveillance of populations, and for the keeping of extensive and often unsuspected records on individual persons. It is now quite possible for one person or agency to assemble a very comprehensive file of information on another individual, without the subject of the information knowing the identity of the knower(s), or anything at all (let alone a comparable amount) about him, her, or them. The subject may well not even be aware of the existence of the data or its possessor, though the possession and subsequent use of the information may affect the life of that person, sometimes drastically.

For all I have talked about the traditional kind of pattern as one in which personal information which is known at all has a common character, there is one exception. In nearly all cultures and societies there is some governing body, other than the "immediate locus of officialdom," whose agents will possess or have access to information about individuals which is by no means reciprocal in the way I have outlined. Government, civil service, police, and other security forces tend always to have access, as part of the apparatus of government, to information in a manner which tends to be one way. Once again, however, we find that this tendency is inevitably multiplied many-fold when modern information technology is employed as part of this apparatus. We shall see a great deal more about this in chapter 3.

My next task here is to look at something of the machinery (both literally and figuratively) of what I have so far been referring to by the blanket term "information technology." What facts justify all the fuss? Who keeps records about us? What machines and systems make this possible and how do they operate? What are the dangers involved and in what general ways do they pose an ethical problem to us? I shall take these questions roughly in order.

The Users

What can be said, first of all, about the locus in society of the phenomenon we are talking about? Who gathers, stores, and makes use of information about us as ordinary citizens, using computerized systems for the purpose? The question can be answered almost as simply as this. Think of anybody whose profession involves "working with people" or "dealing with the general public" in such a way that an individual client or customer needs sometimes to be reidentified. Nearly all of these people will possess or have access to electronically stored information on those clients or customers. This includes not only those who deal with us face to face, but also the vast army of behind-the-scenes workers including, most significantly, those in positions of power and authority in the agencies or companies in question. Even the clause "in such a way that an individual client or customer needs sometimes to be reidentified" is coming to rule out much less than it once did, as we make more of our casual purchases through credit arrangements with stores or mail-order companies.

Government agencies are perhaps the most obvious place to expect that such records will be found. The nature and variety of these agencies varies from one country to another, but will usually include such departments as central records office, vehicle licensing, state education, police and perhaps other security forces, maybe welfare services, and probably a number of others with which a smaller proportion of the population will need to come into contact (not that the absence of contact on the individual's part is guaranteed to mean the absence of records).

Apart from government agencies, there will also be a host of other concerns, either commercial or otherwise, which monitor various aspects of our lives or at least our dealings with them. These include employers, banks, insurance and pension schemes, services such as gas, water, electricity, and telephone companies, mortgage companies, some large stores, credit agencies, and trade unions and professional associations.

Nor, as we shall see shortly, is it just the number of such records which there is reason to find worrying. The way in which information is stored in our microchip world makes it simple for information to be passed around from one user to another, or put together to form a more comprehensive picture of the individual than was contained in any single file. Thus the number of such files which exist in various locations takes on a dimension which is not merely quantitative. Naturally not everyone who has access to computerized information on individuals is in a position to perform such operations with it or to pass it on to anyone else electronically. Those who do have such capability, however, are usually those with the greatest motive for doing so, or a vested interest in the outcome. This is something which I shall be looking at in more detail later.

Other Concerns

Anxieties about computers and information technology are not, however, limited to fears regarding personal privacy and the effects on individual freedom and political liberty. There is also legitimate cause for concern over such issues as whether computers are necessarily error-prone in ways which are threatening to us, whether or not we are faced with the prospect of a society in which day-to-day life is "dehumanized" by technology, the effects which computerization and information technology might have on our understanding of such concepts as those of property and ownership, and some others. When a new set of human capabilities becomes manifest, when we are presented with a whole range of hitherto unexplored techniques in the way in which information technology now appears to be equipping us, the ramifications are never easy to pin down. The one thing which is, perhaps, certain is that they will outstrip the possibilities which have previously been foreseen, and that their implications will exceed those which have been anticipated at the time of their implementation. The most we can do is to make some intelligent guesses at the variety of potential problems, puzzles, enigmas, and dilemmas which will emerge. To do so is inevitably risky; not to do so, however, is downright irresponsible. It must not, therefore, be thought surprising if some of what follows appears as a stab in the dark. Stabs in the dark are, on the whole, better than no stabs at all.

Leaving such concerns until later, I now turn to a brief survey of what lies at the heart of all the problems — the computer itself. Following this, I shall attempt to throw some light on the connection between the nature of the technology as such, and the nature of the moral problems to which it may be seen as giving rise.

The Nature of the Beast

A computer is, at the very least, a machine which is able to receive input in the form of data, to store and process this data according to a program, and to produce something as *output* in consequence. A distinction is sometimes made between "data" and "information," according to which data is pure ground-level "facts," especially as stored in a way which is understandable to a machine, and information is material in a form which is meaningful to human beings, and especially that which has been interpreted in some way, as opposed to being "raw data." The two terms are not always used in just this way, nor will we be adhering rigidly to this usage; where the distinction is important, attention will be drawn to it. One aspect of it is important here, however, and forms a good starting point for this section. The language which the computer actually "understands" (known as its "machine language" or "machine code") cannot be read, except with the utmost difficulty, by human beings — even those who habitually work with computers — since it employs the binary notation consisting only of the symbols 0 and 1. How, then, do persons and machines communicate with each other? The answer is, via a programming language. Programming languages contain some words which are like words in ordinary English, as well as symbols and other bits of jargon. They can be learned without too much trouble by human beings, and can be handled by the machine, which translates them into its own machine language before doing anything with what it receives. The machine will only accept as input that which is couched in a formal language, though it will (somewhat unfairly, perhaps) itself often give its output in something like normal English.

The idea of a program, mentioned above, is crucial to understanding what makes a computer a computer. The program tells the computer what it is supposed to be doing with what the user puts into it. This is how the machine "knows" whether one is typing in a list of prices to be added together, a list of temperatures to make into a graph, or a poem for syntactic analysis. A machine which is not programmable is not normally called a computer, but tends to be named according to the task it performs, such as "calculator." Non-programmable machines perform only a single task or small range of tasks as their total repertoire. Thus a pocket calculator can be given different equations to solve, but solving equations is all it will do. One cannot, for instance, get it to answer yes/no type questions, or to ask questions itself. A machine which is programmable, however, can be made to perform all sorts of operations depending on what program it receives, and this versatility is largely responsible for the features which interest us here. The other significant difference from our point of view between a computer and any other kind of machine is that a computer will have an extensive *memory*, allowing data to be stored automatically in large quantities. This is divided into the main memory (in the machine itself) and the backing store (tapes, disks, and so on). It is processed in the control unit (which handles the carrying-out of instructions from the program) and the arithmetic-logic unit (which performs calculations). The main memory, control unit, and arithmetic-logic unit are collectively known as the central processing unit or CPU.

Input can take a variety of forms, such as a keyboard or more long-established devices, such as punched cards. An "interactive" machine has a visual display unit, or VDU, consisting of a keyboard plus screen, so that the user can talk to the machine and read its output at the same time. Most modern computers are of this kind. On some older types of machine the output also may take the form of cards or tape. All machines have the capacity to give "hard copy" on paper when linked up to a printer. The fixed parts which the computer has, whatever is being done on it, are the "hardware," and the programs which are interchangeable depending on purpose are called the "software."

A significant development from our point of view is the sending of input and the reception of output via *telecommunications*. Networks of computers can be built up, each capable of outputting to, and receiving input from, the others by means of telephone cables or radio signals.[4] Such networking makes possible the transferring, compiling, and comparison of data over long distances very quickly and efficiently. This feature will, of course, loom large in what follows, insofar as it is true of data concerning human beings.

From Computers to Databases

Although there is a strict sense of "computation" according to which what goes on at the micro-level is a kind of computation, what the computer does for us as users is much broader than mere calculation. A large part of it consists in the systematic storage of data in a form that can be retrieved selectively according to the requirements of the user. An arrangement of data in the computer's memory in this fashion is called a *database*, and the notable characteristic of a database is that the data it contains can be accessed in a whole variety of different ways. Suppose we have a list of different pieces of information all related to each other in various respects, for example, a list of names, addresses, and telephone numbers. One thing which we could do with this list would be to store it (either in a computer's memory or elsewhere) just as it stands — as a mere list. If we did this, every time we wanted to find some piece of information, such as how many of the telephone numbers begin with a 6, or whether there is anybody with the surname Chuzzlewit in the list, we would have to look through the entire list. A computer database, however, can be interrogated in such a way that the machine itself will perform such tasks for us, and will do it in a fraction of the time it would take a human being to do the same thing. The relevance of this to our present subject of inquiry should be obvious. For we can extend this simple list with three parameters to a list containing the names of thousands of individuals, even millions. And the number of parameters (name, address, telephone number, and so forth) can be increased on a similar scale. The result is that if we want, say, the names of all the black chefs over 40 and under six feet tall living in a certain district, then, provided all the relevant information is contained somewhere in the list, we can get what we want within seconds. It is, at least in part, the idea of a database (and of a data bank — an agency which deals in database-held information) that has given present-day data technology its power both for doing good and for doing harm.

It makes sense at this point to discuss the difference between a common computer and a database that makes the latter such an alarming prospect. A database is not a type of computer (though there are machines designed specifically to support databases). Nor, on the other hand, is it a piece of software which enables a computer to perform some particular task or other, though there is software aimed at database use, for example, database management systems. Rather, it is a total system consisting of the machine or machines themselves, the software which makes them run, and the data stored in them. A leading authority on databases has defined them as follows:

> A database system is basically a computerized record-keeping system — that is, a system whose overall purpose is to maintain information and to make that information available on demand.[5]

It might further be pointed out that databases involve a basic difference of approach from that found in computing generally. In most areas of computing the general strategy is, to use a common phrase, "program-centered," while that of database technology is "data-centered." In other words, while most computer specialists regard their software as the central part of their work, and the data (input and output) as merely by the way, database specialists tend to see the software as secondary, and the data itself as what really counts. Nor is this surprising, since not only is the data in a database residual and not transitory, it is also expensive — far more expensive than the software, and often more so than the machines themselves.

One reason why the data represents a large amount of capital is the sheer quantity of it which can be held in an average database. A size of 10,000 megabytes (a megabyte being one million bytes, or eight million binary digits of data), for example, is not unusual. Another is the fact that the relevant data is often difficult to come by in the first place. When a database is set up, the information which initially goes into it must come from somewhere, and this is usually from the files of other agencies. Agencies, of whatever kind, are reluctant to give up their information to have it made available — even for perfectly harmless purposes — in someone else's database and at someone else's discretion. For this reason it is often said that the work of setting up a database is 90 percent political and only 10 percent technical.

Once a database is set up and working it is updated regularly, so that its usefulness increases with its lifespan. In order that no inconsistencies can arise within the database (for example, a figure's being altered in one place but not in another), the rule of "one fact in one place" is rigidly insisted upon. This feature of database organization is described by saying that a database should be integrated. Besides absence of duplication, the organization of a database should aim at the elimination of redundancy and the maintenance of standards (in the sense of holding all information in the same kind of notation, all quantities in the same units). A database typically makes it possible for many users to have access to the same store of information without inconveniencing each other. But besides being designed to make information readily available to users, a database is also constructed with the purpose of preventing the information within it from getting into the wrong hands. This is the aspect of security, which will also have an obvious relevance to much which will be said later.

Most modern databases are of the kind known as relational, though there exist other kinds, such as the hierarchical and the network. A relational database holds all its information in the form (as far as the user is concerned) of tables. The user can inspect these tables, produce permutations of them, and abstract certain features from them. As an example, consider the following table of students, containing the registration number of each, his or her name, age and subject. Let us suppose that it is contained in a computer file called STUDENTS:

NUMBER	NAME	AGE	SUBJECT
1	Copperfield	18	French
2	Nickleby	25	Archaeology
3	Rudge	21	Music
4	Chuzzlewit	28	Classics
5	Drood	19	History

This is precisely the kind of table which might occur in a relational database. Now, if I wish, in database terminology, to "interrogate" the database, I may, for instance, give it the command "SELECT Name, Subject FROM STUDENTS WHERE age > 21." What this means, in ordinary English, is "Take from the file called STUDENTS the name and subject of all those whose age is over twenty-one." In response to this request I will receive the following table extracted from the above:

NAME	SUBJECT
Nickleby	Archaeology
Chuzzlewit	Classics

This is precisely what I asked for. Now imagine this kind of capability, only on a far, far vaster scale, involving millions of names, with hundreds of features recorded against each name.

So far we have looked a little at the capacities of computerized systems themselves, but not at the gathering of information which is to be fed into the machine, nor at the use of the information derived as output. These will enter the picture in the next section, in which the kind of system described above can give rise to some of the ethical problems described in the remainder of this book.

The Ethical Dimension

Why should there be any danger, much less a moral problem, about consigning facts to machines, even when these are facts about ordinary, innocent people? Does it not simply mean that the data involved should be stored and manipulated more efficiently and economically than it could be otherwise? Let me begin by tracing the path of such data through the typical system from input to output, and seeing what kinds of moral issues arise at each stage of the process.

First comes the business of actually gathering the information which is to be stored. It might be thought that the way this is conducted has nothing to do with the problems with which we are concerned, for the actual collecting of facts is rarely done by the machine itself but is the work of human agents. However, even here the influence of the technology is at work. The attitudes of those who decide upon the means and the extent of such information-gathering are unavoidably colored by knowledge of the way in which the information is to be stored and processed. These facts about the machine can be divided into two kinds: facts about what the machine can do and facts about what the machine must do — what it makes possible and what it makes necessary.

With reference to the former, if we know that the information collected is to be kept in a form which allows for practically unlimited storage space, and if we also know that more information will not mean greater difficulty of access and retrieval, then we will be tempted to do more extensive and therefore perhaps indiscriminate data collection than we would otherwise. The ease and economy of modern data storage means that the collection of large amounts of information with no immediate application ("just in case") becomes more attractive. When the information concerned is personal information about people, it is easy to see why this practice should be found worrying.

With regard to the latter point, the computer does have its limitations, and one of these is its inability to receive information except in the limited variety of forms which it happens to understand. These are determined by the program in the way described a few pages back. Further limitations may be imposed by the very size of the file in question and the need to arrange it in a way which allows for ease of retrieval. The result is that information has to be standardized to fit a predetermined pattern. Most people will be familiar with the kind of form which one is obliged to complete, and into which none of the relevant information will fit properly. Consider the following example:

1.	SURNAME	⬚⬚⬚⬚⬚⬚⬚⬚⬚
2.	FORENAMES	⬚⬚⬚⬚⬚⬚⬚⬚⬚⬚⬚⬚
3.	MARRIED OR SINGLE? (Write M or S)	⬚
4.	PRESENT EMPLOYER (If unemployed write "unemployed")	
		⬚⬚⬚⬚⬚⬚⬚⬚⬚⬚⬚⬚⬚

This will cause problems for some people attempting to complete it. For example, many oriental people have a family name which precedes their own individual name. Thus the surname *is* the forename. Widowed or divorced persons would have trouble with the third item, while someone with a private income would not fit properly into either of the categories allowed in the fourth. A Chinese widow of independent means would probably have thrown the document away already. It is not only computerization which gives rise to this narrowness of approach, and neither are all computerized documents as narrow as the above. The need to handle large amounts of information often requires a certain uniformity of presentation. Yet undeniably the advent of machine storage has given this trend a distinct push. If a document is to be read by a human being, it is always possible to cross out a question, give an unexpected answer, or add a footnote. In most cases, the machine would simply ignore these expedients. The result is what is sometimes referred to as dehumanization: no clear picture of an individual is ever really built up, since the systems require concentration on the ways in which people are alike, at the expense of those things which make people significantly different from each other. I shall say more about dehumanization later on.

The second step, after the gathering of information, is its storage in mechanical form. Here the same considerations apply as in the gathering stage, in that the stored data is arguably more likely to be indiscriminate and standardized if the storage process is computerized.

Indiscriminacy means an amount of data which is disproportionate to the purpose it is intended to serve. But there are further considerations at this stage. The most important arises out of a crucial difference between storage in a computer's memory and any other kind of storage. Take human memory, for example. We remember certain facts for certain lengths of time: if they are important to us we are more likely to remember them than if they are incidental, and if there are only a few items we will remember them more easily than we would a long list. For these very reasons we may commit information which we wish to be preserved to paper in the form of record cards or notebooks. These forms of records, however, are also bound to be severely limited in capacity when compared with a powerful computer, and the result of this is that a careful eye must usually be kept on the amount of information which continues to be stored. Records are destroyed when they become out of date or no longer useful — often simply to create space for new ones. Sometimes they just get lost. By contrast, the computer's memory, if we include potential storage on disk or tape, appears practically limitless. A single disk (a hard disk, and not the home computer's "floppy") is capable of holding up to 20 million bytes (memory units) of data, which is equivalent to maybe 4 million English words — more than five and a half times the size of the Bible! A disk of this kind takes up very little space when it is not doing anything, compared to the space which would be occupied by the corresponding amount of data stored in more traditional forms. The effect of this massive and normally efficient storage capacity is often that data is kept in such a form for far longer than its useful life. (Anyone who has worked with computer files will be aware of the tendency to concentrate on what *is* immediately important, at the expense of the out-of-sight filestore which is not currently relevant.) This means (a) that the information itself is likely to become inaccurate and out-of-date if not regularly updated, and (b) that even if it remains accurate, the purposes for which it was originally required will eventually become outdated. In either case we have a problem regarding the increased opportunity for the intentional or unintentional perpetration of injustices. Furthermore, computerized records are such that their subject may very well be unaware of their existence, and so is unlikely to see or have any opportunity of correcting them. This point will surface again at a later stage.

The third step is that of the processing of information once it is stored in electronic form. Here two complementary features stand out. First, there is the potential for compiling isolated pieces of information into a large and integrated file. Whereas with manual records it would be a mammoth task to turn up (for example) every reference to a particular person in all the files of all the agencies in a particular region, and compile them in a systematic way to form a complete picture of what is known about that person, with computer files this would be relatively easy. The software tends to be designed for just this sort of purpose. Files can easily be listed, compared, and merged. This makes otherwise harmless pieces of personal information much more important when recorded in sufficient quantities. Many encroachments on the freedom and privacy of individuals which result from computerized data do not occur through the acquiring of particular pieces of especially significant or intimate information, but by the assembling of a lot of bits of information which, taken on their own, are both trivial and readily available. One way in which the transition from manual to computerized record keeping brings about this effect is by breaking down a distinction which is of the greatest importance to us here. This is between two sorts of record keeping: the *demographic* form and the *dossier* form. Demographic records hold statistical information on whole groups of people: for example, the fact that 23 percent of a given population are divorced. This is, of course, built up from bits of information about individual persons from the findings of survey and census takers — for instance, that Mr. X is divorced, that Ms. Y is not, and so on (and the persons themselves might be anonymous right from the start). The point is that, provided the findings are used for demographic purposes and not as personal files on individuals, most of us are not too worried (though some people do object to census questionnaires in the, often mistaken, belief that they will be used as personal files). The dossier form, on the other hand, does not record the incidence of a particular feature over a group of people, but the particular features of each person in the group. A simple illustration will clarify this distinction. The following tables are examples of demographic and dossier forms of record on the same group of people, and with respect to the same features of those people.

Notice that whilst all the information in the left-hand table could be gleaned from the right-hand table, the reverse is not the case. But if we are primarily interested in overall statistics, we would store the information in demographic form, as in the left-hand table, and forget which persons had which characteristics. We would not want the job of having to keep two sets of records, or of having to work out all the averages and percentages every time we needed them. But with the technology now

DEMOGRAPHIC	DOSSIER
Sample: Mr. A, Ms. B, Mr. C, Ms. D, Ms. E	Mr. A: Age 20, married, 1 child
Average age: 30	Ms. B: Age 33, married, 2 children
Proportion married: 40%	Mr. C: Age 37, single, no children
Proportion divorced: 20%	Ms. D: Age 42, divorced, 2 children
Average number of children: 1	Ms. E: Age 18, single, no children

at our disposal we can easily keep information in dossier form in the knowledge that the machine will work out the statistics for us any time, at the drop of a hat. Thus the pressure to keep personal files is increased, even where it is not information on individuals *as* individuals which is the primary object.

The other, and in a way opposite, factor at this stage is the ease with which we can pick out, or abstract, a particular piece of information from a bulky and comprehensive set of data not necessarily designed for that purpose. To extract a list of all the people in Boston whose children have ages totaling 25 would be a well-nigh impossible task using manual records, even given that all the relevant information was there in the first place (unless, of course, this very fact about each person happened to have been entered in its own right, in which case it would still be a Herculean task). But provided the information was in some way contained in the given data, a computer could quite easily sift it out. A reader with some elementary knowledge of programming could probably work out how it might be done; the reader with a more extensive acquaintance will probably have done so already. The relevance of this feature for ethical problems relating to surveillance and control should be fairly obvious.

The fourth stage in the sequence is that of retrieval. Here again, two complementary factors present themselves. On the one hand, retrieval of information from a computer is very easy indeed, with no need for leafing through books and ledgers, no question of painstakingly copying or even typing out the information by hand. We key in a few simple formulae, and the machine will do all the rest for us. On the other hand, it is only easy for those who have access to the machine and who know how to operate it or are in a position to get someone to do it for them. Even the easiest technique is useless to the person prevented from applying it, and the simplest formula is no help to a person who does not understand it or know what it is. In this way it is made easier for those with access to computers and data banks (nearly always those people "on the inside" of some organization or other) to gain access to information on other people and sometimes to use it for their own ends. At the same time, the information is kept in a form which is often inaccessible to the subject of it, both in the sense that that person does not have physical access to it (which could be equally true of manually kept records) but also as a result of the fact that he or she probably does not even understand the form in which they are kept, and must rely on those "on the inside" to act as oracle. The fact that computers, however prevalent nowadays, are the natural province of only a small proportion of the population is very often overlooked in discussions of these issues.

Two words of warning here. First, it is neither as fashionable nor as easy as it once was to believe that an individual's right of access to files on him or herself is going to make a significant contribution in practice to the prevention of injustices. A recent writer on the subject observes:

> Ever since the computer became a major force in the administration of large government and business organizations in the mid-1960s, the individual's right to see and correct his own computerized record has been held up as a miracle cure for many of the potential abuses of the computer age. . . . The principle was subsequently embraced by both the Privacy Act of 1973 and the 1977 report of the Privacy Protection Study Commission. . . . But the [Office of Technology Assessment] report indicating that more than half of the millions of criminal history records now circulating in the United States are incomplete, inaccurate or ambiguous is compelling evidence that the remedies prescribed by law and regulation are not very effective.[6]

Secondly, there is an important aspect of the problems connected with information retrieval which nevertheless seems to me to have only an indirect and (despite its intrinsic importance) incidental bearing on the ethical issues we are considering. This is the enormous area of data security. I shall be saying a great deal about data *protection*, but relatively little about data *security*. Roughly the difference is that the former is to do with what principles, legal or otherwise, should be observed with regard to the availability of information, while the latter is about preventing people from violating those principles once adopted. Data security is concerned with locks and bolts, codes, personnel cards, passwords, and so on. The only ethical problems here relate to such things as a company's duty to individuals whose records they keep to install adequate data security techniques, what to do in the light of the fact that no security system is foolproof, and other issues in which the actual business of data security plays only a supporting role.

The fifth and final stage is that of the use of the information retrieved. Like the gathering of information, this might seem at first sight to have little to do with the electronic form in which the information has been stored, but it turns out to have a great deal to do with it. The ease of access and difficulty of security in computerized systems makes it much simpler for the "wrong" people to get hold of it. What we might mean by the wrong people will be discussed later, especially in chapters 5 and 6. Furthermore, the fact mentioned earlier in this section, that computerized records are likely to be unknown to the subject, means that there is also more opportunity for the information in question to be used covertly as well. This is all too often the case.

Here is a list of the considerations that are likely to cause the kinds of ethical problems to be discussed in later chapters:

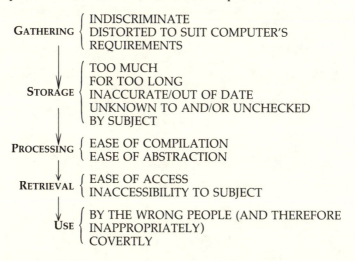

GATHERING { INDISCRIMINATE
DISTORTED TO SUIT COMPUTER'S
REQUIREMENTS

STORAGE { TOO MUCH
FOR TOO LONG
INACCURATE/OUT OF DATE
UNKNOWN TO AND/OR UNCHECKED
BY SUBJECT

PROCESSING { EASE OF COMPILATION
EASE OF ABSTRACTION

RETRIEVAL { EASE OF ACCESS
INACCESSIBILITY TO SUBJECT

USE { BY THE WRONG PEOPLE (AND THEREFORE
INAPPROPRIATELY)
COVERTLY

What I have said in this section, and what is embodied in the above diagram, is a set of tendencies, often unsuspected by those unused to the application of computers, which ought to be fairly obvious when pointed out. They are perhaps harmless enough taken separately, but assume a more alarming aspect when viewed together; they arise out of the current prevalence of information technology, and in one form or another give rise to the moral problems in which I am interested. The above is very incomplete and does not cover all the issues which will be discussed later in this book, but it provides a jumping-off point for many of the areas with which I shall be dealing.

Furthermore, while the above might furnish a useful outline from the point of view of the systems engineer, it is not so appropriate a classification for the purposes of moral philosophy. I have selected those features of modern information technology which give rise to moral problems, and not the problems themselves. For this reason, I have not arranged any of the succeeding chapters according to this scheme. Rather, they focus on the apparent areas of moral concern themselves, which often cut across the categories used in this little outline.

2. Technology as Morally Neutral

The last chapter touched on the question of what an appropriate ethical response would be to a change in the factual circumstances, such as the kind of change with which I am concerned. It was suggested that, although it is reasonable to talk of moral ideas changing and developing over periods of time as a reaction to a changing world, we must be careful how we express this. One thing which I claimed cannot be the case, is that our response must be to rethink our fundamental values from scratch — for this cannot be done. Nietzsche's "revaluation of values" and Skinner's behavioral conditioning only make sense against an existing background of reasons. Another way of expressing this is to say that, though values have something to do with facts (perhaps with facts, for example, about the kind of creatures which we, as human beings, are), we cannot simply "read off" values from facts. We cannot, for instance, say, as people sometimes do, that for a high-tech world we need a high-tech outlook, if this is meant to include our entire moral outlook as well as everything else.

It is now time to look in more detail at how the technological developments I am discussing connect with the context of moral action and appraisal. It makes sense to begin by asking a little more about what relation is supposed to exist between a moral judgment, or an action which is a result of one, and the context of "hard facts" within which it is made or performed. This is too large a question to deal with here in its entirety, and I shall look at only one aspect of it. This involves drawing the following distinction, which will be relevant to some of what comes later in the chapter.

Tools Versus Constraints

Broadly speaking, there are two ways in which facts have to be taken into account in the making of moral decisions. On the one hand, what decision should be taken in a given situation depends on the circumstances in the sense of what we can do. It is no good replying to someone wondering whether or not to cooperate with a fascist government by saying, "Overthrow it" — the choice might well be between collaboration and martyrdom. Nor is it possible to treat a person who has the power to begin a nuclear war as though this need not figure in his moral calculations any more than it need in mine. What *tools* are available to us alters our scope of moral action. As many moral philosophers have pointed out, "ought" implies "can"; and we might add, "can" implies "ought to take seriously into account."

The second way in which hard facts enter into moral decision-making is as a background to action. We make decisions in response to particular situations. Specifically we need to take into account those facts which bear on the probable consequences of our actions. If we know with some certainty that the effect of higher interest rates will be increased inflation, or that the result of de-nationalization will be higher rates of unemployment, these facts will form part of the picture, as it were, within which we act and upon which we act.

The two ways in which facts enter into moral decision-making correspond, then, respectively to the notion of a tool, an enabling device, and to that of a constraint, a circumstance which we have to take into account in deciding what to do and which limits and guides our choice of action or judgment. This is a rather rough-and-ready distinction: some facts will fall on neither side of it (being simply irrelevant), others may fall on both sides, and sometimes the distinction might break down altogether. Its purpose will, however, become clear in a moment.

The Idea of Moral Neutrality

The point of the above is to make it possible to understand a particular way of looking at the rise of information technology and its proper place in our moral thinking — a way which we will have to take very seriously. It centers around the idea that *the technology itself is morally neutral*. The essence of this view is the contention (or more often the assumption) that, while information technology is a useful tool, either for good or bad purposes, depending on our choices, it does not materially alter the world in which we live, at least from a moral point of view — that is, it does not constitute a constraint in the above sense. A defender of this outlook is likely to say something like: Yes, computers and suchlike are relevant insofar as we can use them to good or bad effect, but they don't really make any difference to the complexion of the world within which we act — in other words, our options remain the same, though our ways of implementing them have altered, potentially either for the better or for the worse. The remainder of this chapter will be concerned with formulating an answer to this challenge.

The appeal of the idea as formulated above lies largely in the popular idea that science is morally neutral — a contentious enough claim in itself, and even more so when transferred to technology. In what sense might science be said to be morally neutral? The answer to this will depend on whether we are thinking of science as a body of knowledge, or of science as an activity. It is clear that both ways of looking at science are current in the way people talk. By the word science some people will mean the sum total of what we currently know, or think we know, about the world (as in "science tells us that matter is energy"), while others will mean that activity which produces the knowledge (as in "science requires observation and experiment").

Now to say that an activity is morally neutral might mean one of two things:

(a) that it is neither good nor bad in itself, so that, other things being equal, no one should be praised or blamed for doing it, or
(b) that there is no morally right or wrong way of doing it, and therefore that what goes on within this activity is not, as such, open to moral approbration or condemnation.

The former kind of claim is the sort which might be made, for example, about playing chess. Unlike committing murders or doing famine relief, there is nothing either morally virtuous or the reverse about it: it makes no moral difference to anything (unless, like Nero's fiddling, we do it to the exclusion of things we ought to be doing). An activity may, however, be morally neutral in the first sense, without being so in the second, and this is arguably the case with science. Although embarking on scientific enquiry is neither a morally good nor bad thing in its own right, once we have embarked on it it makes a great moral difference how we go about it, particularly with regard to our purposes in pursuing our enquiries — what we want to prove (if anything) and why. Much controversy, for instance, has surrounded attempts to measure the relative intelligence of black and white people. Why, we may ask, with so many useful lines of enquiry to pursue, should anyone be so interested in this one? This is not to say that there can be no good answer to such a question — only that we are entitled to ask it. Scientists do not, whatever some people would like to think, choose their research projects in a kind of social vacuum, or haphazardly at random. If something presents itself as interesting to a person, this is the beginning, and not the end, of the question concerning why it appeals to him. Thus motives for doing particular things within the activity can be either laudable or suspect. And incidentally, anyone who is tempted to think that the decision to take up science in the first place is praiseworthy in itself is probably associating the decision with certain kinds of motive — medical research or third-world development, for example — and not some other such as chemical warfare or brainwashing techniques!

So much for science as an activity. What people have in mind when they speak of the neutrality of science is not, however, usually the interests and specializations of particular scientists, but the body of knowledge to which scientific activity gives rise. There is certainly some truth in the idea that knowledge is morally neutral, if this is taken to mean that it acquires a morally significant effect only through the way it is used, and that a given piece of knowledge can be used in an endless variety of different ways. Thus the same facts are just as apt for creating poisons as antidotes, power stations as missiles. Facts, in this sense, cannot in themselves be either good or bad from a moral point of view — they are simply facts. But if it is the use made of facts which alone introduces the moral dimension, is this not surely the role of technology? For is technology not essentially the putting into practice of scientific knowledge? Unfortunately even this will not quite do, as we shall see.

Science Versus Technology

The naive position regarding the relationship of science to technology goes roughly as follows. Science is pure, disinterested enquiry, independent of any prospective application of the knowledge to which it gives rise. Scientists typically spend their time working on such projects as the theory of relativity or the principles of quantum mechanics. Technology, on the other hand, is precisely that enterprise which aims at concrete results. This may involve taking the principles discovered by scientists and "applying" them in the pursuit of these results. For example, a technologist might be someone who applies the laws of aerodynamics to produce guidelines for aircraft construction.

Much has already been written about this distinction. The commonest criticism of it is probably the (allegedly spurious) prestige which it tends to lend to "pure" as opposed to "applied" science, i.e., technology. Peter Medawar has suggested that this feature is actually a corruption of a quite legitimate distinction which has come down to us largely from Francis Bacon:

> Bacon's distinction is between research that increases our power over nature and research that increases our understanding of nature, and

he is telling us that the power comes from the understanding . . . no one now questions Bacon's argument. Who nowadays would try to build an aeroplane without trying to master the appropriate aerodynamic theory? Sciences not yet underpinned by theory are not much more than kitchen arts. Aeronautics, and the engineering and applied sciences generally, do of course obey the Baconian ruling that what is done for use should so far as possible be done in the light of understanding. Unhappily, Bacon's distinction is not the one we now make when we differentiate between the basic and applied sciences. The notion of *purity* has somehow been superimposed upon it, and in a new usage that connotes a conscious and inexplicably self-righteous disengagement from the pressures of necessity and use. The distinction is not now between the empirically founded sciences and those whose axioms were supposedly known a priori; rather it is between polite and rude learning, between the laudably useless and the vulgarly applied, the free and the intellectually compromised, the poetic and the mundane.[1]

Yet this idea of the relative prestige of science and technology is not the only extraneous notion with which the Baconian distinction has become encrusted. At least as misleading is the popular idea, embodied in the "naive" view above, concerning the kinds of motivation proper to science and technology respectively. For to regard "real" science as essentially pure, disinterested enquiry is to suggest that the motives by which pure scientists are actuated have nothing whatever to do with intended or foreseen outcomes. A genuine scientist, according to this naive picture, is a person who becomes interested in this or that line of enquiry for no apparent reason at all, and whose interest is entirely self-sustaining: a person whose intellectual tastes and preferences are quite divorced from any recognizable human motives, such as the wish to make life easier or safer, or to make the world a more agreeable place in which to live. This is, of course, a caricature, as is the whole picture which I have painted of the naive position. Yet I am sure that the picture will be a familiar one.

It should already be apparent what is wrong with this picture. Real science does not conform to this model at all. Even the purest of pure scientists usually has some idea of the kind of practical results which might arise from his or her work. And if the naive view has got it wrong about science, it must also have got it wrong about the relation between science and technology. It is simply impossible to make a rigid distinction based on the notion that the latter activity has practical goals while the former does not. To try and do this leaves science as such with no intelligible rationale. It becomes totally mysterious how anyone could ever acquire an interest in it. In reality the distinction between science and technology is by no means clear-cut. Neither side of the divide could operate without motives and objectives which the naive picture as attributes to the other. Furthermore, it is not this distinction (the distinction between having and not having applications of some sort in mind) which is operating at all. This does not mean that the distinction between science and technology, pure and applied, breaks down altogether. A fuzzy line is still a line; and the fact that one way of drawing the distinction proves inadequate does not entail that none will ever be adequate. How else, then, might it be formulated?

Truth Versus Usefulness

There is a distinction which cuts rather deeper and which also rests on a firmer conceptual foundation than the naive one above. This is the distinction between usefulness and truth. Pure science, according to the view which this suggests, is concerned with deriving statements and theories which are true; it is concerned, in other words, with facts. Technology, or applied science, on the other hand, aims at developing useful techniques. In a nutshell this account tells us that science is to do with knowing that, while technology is concerned with knowing how.

The virtue of this account is that it does not force us to choose on every occasion between the two. It does not compel us to place every piece of research or enquiry into one box or the other. The distinction is not between different individual theories or research programs, but between different aspects of most of them. Clearly many cases of knowing that are also cases of knowing how, and vice versa. Knowing that certain mathematical propositions are true, for example, involves knowing how to perform particular sorts of calculation. Similarly, knowing how to drive a car or program a computer entails knowing some facts, to the effect that if one does this or that, then such-and-such results will follow. Not all knowledge follows this pattern (a person who knows how to perform a high-wire act may well not know the physical facts which underpin it), but enough do follow it to explain the significant overlap between the divergent but closely related enterprises of pure and applied learning.

So striking is the relationship between knowing how and knowing that, between truth and applicability, that some philosophers have suggested that the concept of truth itself is best illuminated by considering the notion of usefulness, in some form or other. These philosophers are known as the *pragmatists*, and the pragmatist school flourished, largely in the United States, in the late nineteenth and early twentieth centuries. Pragmatist theories of truth tend to be chiefly contrasted with correspondence theories (truth is what in fact corresponds to some independent reality), and coherence theories (truth is that which allows us to build a coherent picture of the world). The three names usually associated with pragmatism are William James, C.S. Peirce, and John Dewey. The pragmatist approach is often caricatured as asserting something very crude, such as "truth is what works." That this simple view is false can be seen very easily: two incompatible theories might be equally useful as guides to action, though only (at most) one of them can be true. Of the three, James is perhaps closest to this crude view. He asserts that "the true is only the expedient in the way of our thinking, just as the right is only the expedient in the way of our behaving."[2] Unfortunately, there is a pervasive ambiguity in James's writing. Sometimes he speaks as though truths are useful because they are true, while being verifiable independently of their usefulness. At other times he seems to suggest that truths are somehow manufactured by the process of verification itself. Furthermore, he wants to say that we can accommodate awkward or recalcitrant experiences by adjusting our total system of beliefs in such a way as to preserve consistency within it. In these ways James's writing seems to veer at different times toward both the correspondence and the coherence models of truth.

Peirce's view is perhaps more sophisticated. He claims that truth is that opinion which inquirers, adopting a scientific methodology, will in the long-run agree upon as a settled orthodoxy.[3] Peirce's pragmatism arises at least partly out of his dispositional analysis of belief. That is to say, he regarded beliefs as dispositions to behave in certain ways, rather than as mental states or mental acts. Yet Peirce also wants to say that it is *the way things actually are* which ultimately brings it about that the beliefs of scientific inquirers will in the end converge. In Dewey's opinion we are "warranted in asserting" something, if it is seen to work and to be confirmed in practice. Thus for Dewey the notion of assertability seems to take the place of the concept of truth.[4] Assertable beliefs are then entitled, he says, to be called knowledge. This view runs into more problems than the other two, however. For one thing, it is hard to see how it can make any sense of the idea of truths which have not yet been discovered. And, even more fundamentally, it is difficult to understand what "warranted in asserting" could mean if not "warranted in asserting as true." And if this is indeed how it should be construed, we are still left with the concept of truth as primitive. In summary it is a feature of all the chief pragmatist writers that where they come close to actually *equating* truth with usefulness, or replacing the concept of truth with some other, their theories tend to look thinnest. Where their doctrines are at their most plausible, they are usually found to suggest an underlying correspondence-type theory not far below the surface.[5]

This brief sketch is meant to suggest that, to the extent to which such a theory is genuinely pragmatist, we ought to be very reluctant to accept it. And if this is so, it follows that we are perfectly entitled to continue operating with a distinction between usefulness and truth — a distinction which would inevitably break down if full-blooded pragmatism were correct. There exists one other philosophical threat to this distinction, which ought to be mentioned in passing. This comes from the school of *scientific antirealism*. It is perhaps wrong to refer to this as a school at all, for those who reject scientific realism are by no means all agreed on what they want to put in its place.[6] Realism in science is, very roughly, the view that the concepts employed in scientific theories actually stand for things in the real world. What is so remarkable about that idea? Nothing, except that many people have questioned it, and some influential thinkers have rejected it outright. The logical positivists, whose bent was toward empiricism (i.e., toward an emphasis on the role of direct experience in the acquisition of knowledge) tended to advocate an operational approach to scientific concepts. Operationalism is the methodological theory which wishes to explain such concepts in terms of their connection with first-hand experience — effects on our scientific instruments and ultimately on our sense organs. Some antirealist writers have gone farther and adopted an outright fictionalist approach to scientific concepts. The idea behind such views is that scientific theories often involve operating with concepts which seem to make reference to unobservable entities (forces, electrons, viruses, and the like). For those who like to maintain a close connection between what we can accept as genuinely existing and what we can actually verify at first hand, the antirealist position has proved attractive. On such a view we can happily talk in terms of "theoretical," nonobservable entities which form part of the fabric of our scientific theories, provided we take care not to endow them with the status of real existence: they are to be seen, in other words, as merely theoretical. This approach faces two severe problems. The first is that the borderline between the observable or real and the merely theoretical is not as sharp as the antirealist is apt to suggest. That which is nonobservable today might well be observable tomorrow. Moreover, any account of what constitutes "first-hand" observation is going to be contentious. Does this include seeing things through a window? And if it does, then why not through a telescope, a microscope, an electron microscope, or via a Geiger counter or a radar device? But more importantly, if the antirealist is correct, how does science purport to explain at all? If we are not really claiming that atoms exist, how can the atomic theory of matter do the job it is supposed to do? This problem can be seen by analogy with ordinary, everyday explanations. If the door won't open, we might conjecture that there is a piece of furniture behind it. If, going in through the other door, we discover that there is no piece of furniture blocking it, we abandon that as an explanation — a nonexistent entity cannot play such an explanatory role or even be a candidate for it. What gives scientific antirealism its plausibility is, of course, that there is no "other door": we have no independent access to the real facts of the matter. Yet it is hard to see how this alters the fact that a candidate for an explanatory role must, to at least the same extent, be a candidate for actually existing. This is by no means the last word which can be said about the realism/antirealism controversy. What I hope it shows, however, is that the onus lies quite squarely with the antirealist who wants to deny that the purpose of science is to come up with truths about the world. In any case, the antirealist's position is not as potentially damaging to the truth/usefulness distinction as is that of the pragmatist; for the usefulness with which the antirealist is concerned is only "usefulness for developing a theory," and not practical usefulness in any strong sense.

Limits to Free Choice

I began this chapter from the apparently quite natural suggestion that a sharp distinction can be made between science (that which is independent of applications) and technology (that which "applies" the principles discovered by science). We saw, however, that the two activities are not in practice separable: "pure research" is always motivated by some expectations regarding potential results and their applications. We have seen, however, that a distinction of principle can be made between the activity of aiming at truth and that of aiming at usefulness: there is no reason to think (as an extreme pragmatist would) that they ultimately collapse into each other. Thus, while acknowledging that science and technology are in practice not wholly separable, we can accept that there is a conceptual distinction to be made between that aspect of any enterprise which aims to discovering truths as such, and that aspect which aims at some ulterior goal. This distinction allows us to preserve the intuitive idea from which we began, that there is a genuine difference between pure truth-seeking and the will to manipulate the environment; but it will not commit us to seeing any scientific or technological undertaking as totally immune from moral considerations. It will not, in other words, lead us to think that what is going on, for example, in one laboratory, is open to moral scrutiny, but that what is happening in the next one is not. Any activity, in its former aspect, will be morally neutral in something like the sense outlined earlier, while in its latter aspect it will not be.

It will be appreciated, however, that to say this is not to make a very great concession to the champions of the moral neutrality of research. For on the present view, every enterprise will have a moral dimension to it, for at least the one simple reason that people do not undertake any activity without some kind of motivation, and motivations are always proper objects of moral scrutiny and concern. About conscious motives enough has already been said. Conscious motives, however, are not the only factors which are morally relevant in considering scientific or technological research and development. There are other elements which are both more pervasive and more difficult to uncover, and it is to some of these that I now turn.

So far I have been looking at this topic as though the technology, while perhaps not morally neutral in the sense of being morally irrelevant, were at least neutral in the sense that where it has morally relevant consequences, it is an open question as to the direction in which these consequences are going to operate. In other words, it has been suggested that what is important from our point of view is what is done with the technology, where this is taken to be merely a matter of what human beings choose to do with it. That this is too simple will shortly be apparent.

In the case of science I made a distinction between the idea of science as an activity and science as a body of knowledge, and it was the former which was seen to be inescapably open to moral appraisal, while knowledge considered purely as such may harmlessly be called morally neutral. I may make a corresponding distinction in the case of technology, and distinguish between the activity of technology, what technologists do, their motives, and so forth (which is largely what I have been talking about so far), and the "technology," meaning the artifacts which represent the results of this technology. Yet the parallel seems to end here, and I suggest that herein lies one of the most important differences between what I am inclined to call science and what may be viewed as technology, as characterized above: while the products of science are facts, those of technology are things — the technology itself — and in no sense can the physical manifestations of technology be said to be morally neutral. For not only can they, like facts, natural laws, principles, calculations, and formulae, be used in a variety of ways for good or evil; the end products of our technology are often such as to influence our own decisions about what to do in particular circumstances. How does it come about that mere "things," artifacts, can influence decisions?

Technology as an Active Force

In his book on the First World War, the historian A.J.P. Taylor gives the following account of how the final mobilization of Germany was at least partly dictated by the nature of available technological resources:

> All the European powers had built up vast armies of conscripts. The plans for mobilising these millions rested on railways; and railway timetables cannot be improvised. Once started, the wagons and carriages must roll remorselessly and inevitably forward to their predestined goal. Horses can be swapped crossing a stream; railway carriages cannot. . . . The Russian decision to mobilise threw out the German timetable. If the Germans did nothing, they would lose the advantage of superior speed. They would have to face war on two fronts, not on one; and this, they imagined, they could not win. Either they had to stop Russia's mobilisation at once by threat of war, or they had to start the war, also at once. . . . On 1st August Germany declared war on Russia; two days later, with hardly an attempt at excuse, on France. The First World War had begun — imposed on the statesmen of Europe by railway timetables. It was an unexpected climax to the railway age.[7]

Other examples, perhaps less spectacular, abound in the realm of modern information technology. Such factors fall into what I earlier labeled the category of constraints upon decision-making, and in certain situations they may represent constraints of the most serious kind. They are factors which, while not actually removing our decision from the sphere of free action, alter radically the context of the decision (just as holding a gun to a person's head does not, strictly speaking, remove that person's freedom of choice, but may well determine what it would be rational or desirable to choose given the circumstances).

To begin with, many technological inventions are geared from the start to a particular kind of application, being useful only in warfare, for example, or in agriculture. Such a device we might label *application-laden*, as opposed to *application-neutral*. In this sense information technology appears to be fairly application-neutral, since, as pointed out in the last chapter, information is not itself a kind of specialty but an aspect of all other topics. Thus information technology is applicable in just about every area of human life.

Secondly, some sorts of device will lend themselves not only to specific applications, but to the implementation of particular policies. The possession of certain types of nuclear missile almost commits the possessor to a first-strike policy in the event of a nuclear confrontation, since that is the only kind of policy which makes strategic sense given the nature of the hardware (which is only good for hitting missiles before they have taken off). Devices like this we may call *policy-laden*, as opposed to *policy-neutral*. We see, then, that there is not only one kind of neutrality in question, but at least two — and other classifications could doubtless be applied.

On the whole, the more specific we become about the kind of technology in question, the less likely are we to discover it to be neutral in the above ways. "Information technology" as such is broad enough to be fairly neutral, though, of course, "spy satellites" (a sub-class of information technology) is not. Notice, however, that "weapons systems" is a broader class, though by no means neutral, at least as regards applications. Once again much depends on how we draw our categories.

It is important to recognize that the kinds of neutrality discussed (application neutrality and policy neutrality) are not supposed to be rivals or alternatives to "moral neutrality," but rather ways in which something might or might not be morally neutral, depending upon one's moral attitude to the application or policies in question. (One might, for instance, be morally opposed to what one is committed to by all weapons technology, or opposed merely to first-strike type missiles.) Policies, of course, are likely to be even more open to moral appraisal and criticism than mere applications. In a moment I shall look at two further ways in which the results of actual or potential technology can fail to be neutral (in either of the above aspects), apart from by virtue of the nature of the hardware itself. Sometimes the way in which the available technology is able to influence decision-making arises simply out of the fact that the decision-makers are human and carry with them a fairly predictable repertoire of human responses. In other cases the causes may lie in the specific nature of the society or culture which, along with the availability of the technology, forms the background to the decision in question. I shall briefly take these in turn.

The Human Factor

This phrase embraces those aspects of what might be called "perennial" human nature, which incline us toward certain courses of action whenever they are open to us. I do not wish to get involved here in a drawn-out discussion of the concept of human nature and what it involves. Among those who place a great deal of weight on the notion, there is no universal agreement concerning "the nature of this nature." However, it ought to be clear that there are certain drives and motivations which are almost ubiquitous, and which mankind tends to lose few opportunities of gratifying when the occasion arises. (I must necessarily concentrate here on the more worrying and disagreeable of them, though this is not to deny that there are more attractive ones by which they can be counterbalanced.) When some advance in human capabilities makes possible their gratification on a massive and unprecedented scale, it is tempting, though perhaps misleading, to see something essentially pernicious in the technology itself.

The most striking example of this, prior to the present postwar period, is probably the aftermath of the Industrial Revolution, when captains of industry, including many otherwise civilized and responsible men, were prepared to turn the urban landscape of Europe into what William Morris called "a counting house on top of a cinder-heap" for the sake of the profit motive.[8] For when the opportunity of increased financial return presents itself, and especially when it presents itself as an aspect of "progress," who can humanly turn it down? If the price of failing to compete with rivals by cutting costs is economic ruin, can it be expected that many will choose the latter? Where the perpetrators have been convinced that what they are doing is in the cause of progress, these options cease to be merely temptations or dictates of *force majeur*, and come to be seen as representing a positive good.

Though the profit motive, as we shall see, is conspicuous in the case of our latest revolution — the computer revolution — it is possibly not so much the attraction of profit as that of power which is central to those aspects of the new technology that many people see as the new threat to the civilized order. Power is surely at least as much a primal and deeply rooted object of human fixation as is profit. When the opportunity arises for a person, an interest group, or a government to strengthen its hand by the employment of such methods as electronic data processing, they are rarely seen willingly to forego it. Once again these measures can always be justified by the catch-all plea of progress (a notion about which something will be said later).

Yet there is a limit to the extent to which human nature can be blamed for the ways in which tools are used or misused. Another important factor is the social and cultural background against which the choices are presented.

The Cultural Factor

The debate regarding which features of human beings result merely from their being human (or from being genetically the way they are) and which are "merely" cultural and inculcated by society is old, ongoing, and not to be settled here. Yet wherever anyone judges that the boundary should be properly drawn, one assumes no one will deny that both sets of influences exist.

The assumptions and prejudices of a particular society or culture represent a further way in which the products of technology cannot be simply regarded as neutral tools carrying no presumptions as to how they might be used. Even a device which, considered simply in itself, might be regarded as capable of being deployed in support of an indefinite variety of policies, might, given a particular set of social circumstances or cultural presuppositions, be inexorably destined to further a determinate range of purposes. Even whether a certain form of technology is worth pursuing and funding at all will depend on such factors (you cannot sell nuclear missiles to people who are not interested in fighting wars; and it is hard to keep them from those who are).

These reflections are relevant to many of our concerns in the rest of this book. I shall explain in chapter 3 how a society needs to have become pathological in some way before data technology can begin to act significantly as a force for repression. In chapters 5 and 6 I will note how certain kinds of social organization tend to provide fertile soil for the wholesale invasion of privacy to flourish. In chapter 7 I shall observe how the socioeconomic background creates the conditions under which computerization can tend toward the dehumanization of human life. In chapter 8 I shall argue that problems about ownership raised by information technology are only seriously problematic in the context of a particular background of assumptions, rooted again in a certain sort of culture with which we are familiar. All these facts will serve to remind us of the futility of attempting to study "the effects of information technology" or "the social consequences of computerization" in isolation from a discussion of the existing social and cultural background against which all this is supposed to be taking place. This point will become more clear as we progress.

I have talked about the ways in which decision-making can be radically influenced by:

(a) the nature of the technology itself, which might easily suggest a specific application or policy,
(b) the appeal of some aspect of the technology to a certain element in human nature, and
(c) the coming together of some kind of technology with a particular social or cultural background.

There is in principle a fourth way, and this is the manner in which the technology might appeal, or fail to appeal, to given individuals. Clearly, however, individual dispositions, important as they might be in some respects, cannot be taken into account in a systematic treatment, for the very reason that, to the extent to which they depart from or go beyond the norm, they are by definition not susceptible to generalizations. It is, then, from the above three angles that I shall largely be examining the problems which form the subject matter of the next few chapters. Because this is not itself a technological work, and since human nature is a thing about which I can do little, it will often be the third which will concern me most.

3. Is Big Brother Watching?

The telescreen received and transmitted simultaneously. Any sound that Winston made, above the level of a very low whisper, would be picked up by it; moreover, so long as he remained within the field of vision which the metal plaque commanded, he could be seen as well as heard. There was of course no way of knowing whether you were being watched at any given moment. How often, or on what system, the Thought Police plugged in on any individual wire was guesswork. It was even conceivable that they watched everybody all the time. But at any rate they could plug in your wire whenever they wanted to. You had to live — did live, from habit that became instinct — in the assumption that every sound you made was overheard, and, except in darkness, every movement scrutinised.

George Orwell, *Nineteen Eighty-Four*

This is George Orwell's description of life in the year 1984. As in most futuristic anti-utopias of which Orwell's was the prototype, electronic gadgetry, especially of the kind that deals with personal information about individuals, plays an important part in the government's oppression of the governed. (For some reason, government oppression is the only serious rival to nuclear holocaust in alarmist science fiction — are there no other ways for a society to go under?) Now the year 1984 has come and gone, but the Orwellian nightmare does not seem to have arrived, nor to be quite on the point of emergence. There are, however, certain features of our developing social environment which are thought to give cause for alarm. Before looking at these sources of worry themselves and trying to discover to what extent the anxiety is justified, one general point is in order.

People's knowledge of computer technology is extremely limited. We are frequently told by the media and by advertisers how necessary it is to be "computer literate," capable of operating electronic gadgetry, and to understand the impenetrable jargon in which the "experts" are supposed to converse, or at least to employ someone who does. Yet such knowledge, despite these protestations, is not at all widespread. In fact knowledge of computing in any form is very rare even in the developed countries and among their educated classes. Special training in schools is now doing something to alter this situation, but there is still a long way to go, if we decide to go in that direction. The majority of people rarely or never require such knowledge in their day-to-day life, and the result of making computer training compulsory could well be to create another subject like Latin or Greek for which the average student will find little practical use, which will soon be forgotten (and nothing is forgotten more quickly than unused programming skills), and which will be looked back on as a waste of a lot of time. On the other hand, ignorance is not a virtue, but notoriously gives rise to fear. One aspect of this fear is the much-inflated picture which many ordinary people have of the capabilities of computers, which often amounts to endowing them with human or even superhuman intelligence.

It is important to separate this kind of worry from genuine and well-founded fears about the effects of electronic record-keeping. The instruments of repression in Orwell's imaginary world were not computers, at least so far as we know, though many people seem to equate the one thing with the other. It is only the scale of the Orwellian "telescreen" system which makes it an effective tool of the Thought Police. The machines themselves are merely a kind of closed-circuit television. Let us then leave the world of fiction — however important that fiction may be as a warning to us — and look at some of the facts which lead to apprehension regarding the future of freedom in a data-bank world.

Causes for Concern

These fears typically arise not out of some apocalyptic vision of the future, but out of small, often isolated and disconnected incidents which occur in everyday life. We read in the newspapers of a person being refused a job because of (sometimes erroneous) information which has somehow reached the employer from a police computer. We hear of files inadvertently made accessible to the subject, which turn out to contain personal and unsuspectedly detailed pieces of information apparently unconnected with the legitimate purpose of the records in question. A recent study mentions the following two cases, which are fairly typical of their kind:

A judicial enquiry into Special Branch records compiled by police in South Australia was carried out in 1977. . . . The then Premier, Mr Don Dunstan, subsequently ordered destruction of most of the files when it was discovered that they covered all Labour politicians, half the supreme court judges, all "left" or "radical" university people, all prominent demonstrators, homosexuals, feminists, and divorce-law reformers. . . . Thomas Spohr . . . became one of 2.5 million West Germans in public employment to be screened by Nadis — the computer of the German security service — to ascertain whether they were "hostile" to the constitution. He was dismissed from employment because he had urged people to vote for the legal West German Communist Party, had drawn a cartoon for a communist newspaper, and had come to Scotland to obtain support for his disciplinary court hearing. Half a million West Germans were called to such hearings to account for their actions — following the build-up of dossiers on computer-based and other systems.[1]

The picture that tends to emerge from such sporadic and often anecdotal pieces of evidence is neither that of complete freedom under the law nor that of Orwell's 1984. It is not so much that every action of every person is liable to be scrutinized and immortalized in an electronic memory. It is rather that there is a gray area of action which is within the law but which renders the agent likely to become the subject of extensive records of a particular kind. The existence of these records, even if it does not constitute a harm done to the subject in itself (as I shall argue in chapter 5 that it might) can result in severe damage to a person who is legally innocent. Now *it is part of the ideal of freedom under the law that someone who is not breaking the law should not be penalized,* and that a person's right to do anything which is not illegal should be respected but actively upheld by the law. The kinds of situation discussed above are contrary to the principle of freedom under the law which is supposed to be a constitutional feature of what we call free societies.

While such instances are sufficiently alarming in themselves, they are not the whole story. Civil rights organizations have a certain amount of success in combatting abuses of this kind, changes of government bring about changes of policy, and so on. If it were simply such isolated cases that worried us, the problem would be a tough one, but manageable and relatively straightforward. It would be a matter simply of discovering where and when these abuses occur, and invoking the law, or public opinion, to try and get something done about them. But I am convinced that this is not what people have in mind when they voice anxiety regarding the effects of data technology on civil liberties.

What they have in mind is not a continual emergence of particular abuses to be dealt with, but a general cumulative movement toward a different kind of society in which freedom, privacy, individualism, and other values will be progressively eroded. The trouble here is the vagueness of the picture, and it is an important capacity of the futuristic novelist to be able to sharpen it for us and complete some of the blurred outlines. But we do not just require more than vagueness, we require more than a picture. What is needed is some connection between the impressionistic visions which people are prone to entertain and the more conceptualized terms of reference of the political philosopher or political scientist. In other words, it is not so much a mental picture of a possible future that we need, as a mental map of the varieties of possible futures we wish to avoid.

The Varieties of Evil

Most people, including many who should know better, have a fatal weakness for generalizations; and from some of these generalizations arise a good proportion of the muddles which philosophers are often called on to disentangle. The tendency toward generalization often appears as the desire to see only two sides to every issue, conflating into one all those positions which differ from one's own. Thus, on the one hand, we have "good" government, incorporating freedom, democracy, equality, and all the other good things in life; and on the other, we have "bad" government which is oppressive, tyrannical, totalitarian, and all the other things of which we disapprove. Possible forms and styles of government present themselves to us as lying along a single scale, with Utopia at one end and the Orwellian hell at the other.

It *may* be that there is only one completely good or correct way of being governed. This is unlikely, since there is an enormous variety of cultures in the world and it seems (even without being committed to any extreme form of relativism) that there is no guarantee of moral commensurability between them. That is, different kinds of culture do not simply lie on a scale from good to bad. And, it is reasonable to suppose, a type of government suitable to one culture will not necessarily be appropriate to another. Furthermore, the art of good government would seem to have a lot to do with compromise — not in the pejorative sense of compromising one's principles or character, but in the sense of balancing one claim against another. Freedom often has to be balanced against equality, for example, or justice against compassion. In this sense, government would appear as a balancing activity, rather than a maximizing activity. There may be no single "best" thing to do in any given set of circumstances, and therefore no single best form of government.

However this might be, it is surely even less likely that there is a single way in which the exercise of authority can go wrong. This is a very general point, not restricted to the case of government. Some activities, such as novel-writing, are such that there are many possible ways of doing them well; others, like army drill, have only one correct way, and all other ways are automatically wrong. But it would seem that *no* undertaking is such that there is only one way of doing it badly or of failing in the object.

Moreover, the temptation to lump together all that we disapprove of under one favorite term of dismissal ("communism," "fascism," "imperialism") is an especially dangerous form of this confusion, for it muddles our thinking about what we are attempting to resist and what should be done about it. This is one of the reasons why threats to our way of life which seem obvious with hindsight are often practically invisible to the contemporary observer. If we are constantly on the lookout for something which conforms to our preconceived image of such a threat, composed from a gallery of mental pictures (red flags, brown shirts . . .) we are bound to miss the real thing when it arrives. The next threat is rarely like the last: if it were, it would not be a threat, for it could be nipped in the bud.

What exactly is it that we think might be made more likely by the rise of information technology? One word which we would probably apply unhesitatingly to Orwell's fictional state is totalitarian. A totalitarian regime may be characterized as one which extends the province of government to include every area of the individual's life. The totalitarian state does not want simply this or that from the individual: it wants the person *in toto*. There is also the suggestion that Orwell's state takes the form of a dictatorship, though this is left (perhaps significantly) unclear. The only trace of personality which the regime has is incorporated in the figure of Big Brother. Big Brother is probably best understood as a fiction existing for the purpose of crediting the Party with the last vestiges of a human face. Yet one is still uncertain whether or not there lies behind the image of Big Brother, the Party, and the Thought Police a single leader or not. Totalitarian states in reality have tended to be dictatorial (or autocratic — the difference seems to be only that "dictator" would not be used of an hereditary monarch, however "dictatorial"), and there is a reason for this. Hannah Arendt, in her authoritative study of totalitarianism, says:

> Totalitarian movements are mass organizations of atomised, isolated individuals. Compared with all other parties and movements, their most conspicuous external characteristic is their demand for total, unrestricted, unconditional, and unalterable loyalty of the individual member. . . . Such loyalty can be expected only from the completely isolated human being who, without any other social ties to family, friends, comrades, or even mere acquaintances, derives his sense of having a place in the world only from his belonging to a movement, his membership in the party. Total loyalty is possible only when fidelity is emptied of all concrete content from which changes of mind might naturally arise. The totalitarian movements, each in its own way, have done their utmost to get rid of the party programmes which specified concrete content. . . . Hitler's greatest achievement in the organization of the Nazi movement . . . was that he unburdened the movement of the party's earlier programme. . . . [in Stalin's Russia] the most perfect education in Marxism and Leninism was no guide whatsoever for political behaviour . . . on the contrary, one could follow the party line if one repeated every morning what Stalin had announced the night before. . . .[2]

Totalitarian movements have tended to require some form of charismatic leadership, at least in bringing about their initial successes, since such movements require loyalty, if not that of all the people at least of those who are to form the organizational nucleus; and the kind and degree of loyalty needed tend to be such as are not accorded to mere programs and policies but only to persons. Once established, however, the movement may be able to do without its charismatic leaders, provided it can control the governed in some other way. This is where high technology comes in. At this stage it is at least possible that an efficient system of electronic surveillance, record-keeping, and propaganda could for a considerable time, if not indefinitely, take the place of loyalty as well as of brute force in maintaining a totalitarian government. Totalitarianism and dictatorship, then, are both conceptually distinct and quite possibly separable in practice; and the conditions for having the former without the latter may even be precisely those which are the subject of this book.

If the state which Orwell describes is not a dictatorship, it would seem at least to be an oligarchy, run by and possibly for the benefit of a small inner ring — the officials of the Party. Oligarchies are perhaps more familiar than either dictatorships or totalitarian regimes, and are conceptually distinct from both: a totalitarian state may or may not be oligarchical, and a dictatorship cannot be.

Finally a much weaker concept which is relevant here is that of centralization. There is a sense in which both dictatorial and oligarchical government involve the centralization of power; yet centralization is by no means equivalent to these concepts, or even necessarily closely connected with them. It is, for example, possible for a democratic government to be highly centralized. Totalitarian regimes have tended to be centralized, probably as a result of the way in which they have arisen around a particular leader-figure, and of their emphasis on conformity. Yet here again the connection is an entirely contingent one. The role of centralization is, however, interesting, and I shall say more about it in a moment.

Roots of Oppression

Two things emerge from the previous section. The first is that the supposed threat to political freedom embodied in our new electronic environment begins to look more manageable and less conducive to mental paralysis when broken up conceptually into distinct possibilities or scenarios. Although this leaves us with what looks like a large number of different threats in place of just one, no single one of these has quite the compelling power of the original caricature.

Secondly, we have a distinction between the conditions which might help to bring a repressive political regime to power in the first place, and those which might be instrumental in keeping it there once established. I would now like to try and develop these two points a little further.

A notable feature of Orwell's world is that, in common with many anti-utopias, no more than a vague gesture is made toward explaining how it all came about. We know that at some time in the novel's fictional past there is supposed to have been a revolution, but we do not know whether this is meant to have arisen from a genuine popular movement or whether it is a bit of Newspeak for talking about a seizure of power by a small group. More significantly we are not told whether the technology which now maintains the Party in power existed prior to that event, or whether it was developed and installed for the purpose. In one sense this is irrelevant, for these considerations play no part in the plot of the book; but in another way it is of supreme importance. For the origins of such regimes, both from a large-scale political and a small-scale psychological point of view, are probably the most interesting thing about them. These origins are very often something of a mystery in reality as much as in fiction.

Nevertheless, certain things are to the point here. We have seen that four categories of political situations are conducive to large-scale information technology:

(1) Totalitarianism
(2) Dictatorship
(3) Oligarchy
(3) Centralization

Beginning at the bottom of the list, with centralization, the first thing to notice is that there is an ambiguity in the term which it is easy to exploit intentionally or unintentionally in contexts such as these. It can refer either to an institutional tendency or a geographical one. In the first sense, government is said to be centralized when authority is concentrated in a small number of bodies, a single body, or even in a single individual. In the second sense, a centralized government is one in which most of the decisions, or at least most of the important ones, are taken at the national rather than the regional or local level. The kind of centralization necessary to some types (and perhaps even to most types) of political oppression is the institutional. But the kind of centralization which we associate with the effects of information technology (if we make such an association at all) is surely the geographical. Records are less likely to be kept by local agencies in isolation, and more likely to be held in vast computer networks spread over a much larger area, thus allowing more scope for planning and decision-making on a far broader scale. This trend may be thought undesirable, but it does not in itself constitute a trend toward a repressive style of government. What fosters the confusion between the kind of centralization which is necessary (though, as we have seen, not sufficient) for a government to be dictatorial or oligarchical, and geographical centralization is the very mundane fact that the former always entails the latter. For a single person (or a committee or junta, when it is meeting) can only be in one place at a time, and therefore tends to govern from one place. Since geographical centralization is necessary to institutional centralization, and since institutional centralization is necessary to dictatorial or oligarchical government, it follows that geographical centralization is necessary to these latter. The point is that this goes no way toward establishing a causal connection.

Failing this, what can be said about the provenance of dictatorships and oligarchies considered in their own right? The term oligarchy is not ambiguous like "centralization," but it is nevertheless vague. How few people need to wield what degree of power before they can be said to constitute an oligarchy? Fortunately we do not need to answer this question as it stands. There are two characteristic types of leadership which actually seem to have recurring instances in the real world, and which are both candidates for the title. These are, first, the *junta* which seizes power, typically, as a result of some form of *coup* having overthrown an ailing government of a more conventional kind; and secondly the party, or at least an inner circle of party officials, in a state run by a single party. Reverting to our original question, it is extremely unclear how any amount of computerization of surveillance techniques and records in a society could be instrumental in bringing about the rise of a dictator, a *junta*, or a particular party. The first two styles of government tend, in fact, to be associated rather with backward and undeveloped nations possessed of only fairly crude means of wielding and transferring authority (the Ugandas and Haitis of the world); or with countries in which something is already amiss, leading people to adopt extreme solutions as better than no solutions at all (as in revolutionary Russia or Weimar Germany).

Government by single party is in a different position, for the following reason. I said that it is not easy to see how the kind of technology we are discussing could help to bring about the rise of a particular party. This is different, however, from the creation of a one-party state when the party in question has already come to power by means of the ballot box. I also said at the beginning of this section that the manipulation of information technology is something which is more likely to be an effective strategy for staying in power than for achieving power in the first place. The reason is that persons not already in a position of some considerable influence would not even begin to have access to the sort of methods we would have to talk about. It may well be true that too many people already have access to personal information on others as a result of information technology; but there is an enormous difference between having access to lists of names, addresses, income-brackets, and so on and being able to control the channels of information on the scale necessary to neutralize all political opposition.

How does this relate to our final category at the top of the list, that of totalitarianism? Totalitarianism is not only a distinct concept from the others we have just been considering, but is of a different order altogether. Here let me make a general distinction. On the one hand, our objection to a government or type of government may be on what might be called constitutional grounds. In this case the claim will be that the existing structure of authority or power embodies a form which is unjust or in some other way undesirable. On the other hand, the objection may be on more general moral grounds such that, without necessarily having to take exception to the form of government, opposition can be justified by appealing to some specific and concrete harm which is being caused. While dictatorship and oligarchy are names of particular forms of government (deriving from the ancient Greek classification of constitutions), the concept of totalitarianism relates to the way in which a government conducts itself toward its subjects, without reference to the type of constitution which it exemplifies.

Nevertheless, a totalitarian state is bound in practice to be a one-party state (though the reverse certainly need not be the case). It is inconceivable that a regime demanding total loyalty, claiming absolute authority over every aspect of subjects' lives, should expose itself voluntarily to political opposition. The trouble for anyone bent on inaugurating such a regime is, then, that either a one-party system must be in existence already (as it was for Stalin) or it must as some point be introduced (as with Hitler). And to introduce one-party government before being in complete control will surely be impossible unless there is some strong factor such as a national emergency inclining the population toward accepting such a system. In short, something must have already gone wrong independently in order to put totalitarianism on the agenda in the first place.

It is, therefore, a grotesque exaggeration to suggest that the technology which we now possess, or even of the kind we are likely to possess in the foreseeable future, is going to bring about a revolution in our society in the direction of political oppression *in this sort of way*. Why, then, have so many people been inclined to buy the idea that this is likely? I suggest that it actually has less to do with the present state of technology, or even of politics, than with the trend of political theory, and particularly "popular" political theory during this century. It is true that the last few decades have presented many examples of tyrannical or totalitarian states. Many people would wish to emphasize such examples in support of an extreme cynicism concerning the role of the state and its place in people's lives. Yet, paradoxically, most present-day states are more tolerant, more welfare-oriented, and support a higher standard of living for a larger section of the population than at any other time in history. Though I do not wish to be over-optimistic about the well-meaningness of states and governments, the cynicism does require a little explanation. I will offer one, and I am sure it is not the only, line of explanation.

From Augustine to Orwell: the Fortress and the Prison

Two conflicting theoretical conceptions of the state have influenced Western thinking, especially about freedom and authority, and are still to be found in various forms in the present day. They do not represent clear-cut or fully blown theories but rather two categories into which political theories tend to fall, depending on which conception is at the back of the author's mind. One I will call Aristotelian. In a famous passage Aristotle tells us that the end and aim of the state

> can only be that which is best, perfection; and self-sufficiency is both end and perfection. It follows that the state belongs to a class of objects which exist in nature, and that man is by nature a political animal; it is his nature to live in a state.[3]

Aristotle was talking primarily about the small-scale city-state and not about states as we know them, but the central point is the same. For Aristotle, there is no necessity to explain why humans require social or political organization in the first place: once the above is accepted the question will not arise, though the question of what sort of organization we should have will inevitably arise. In Aristotle's view political order is not something artificially imposed on human beings, nor a mere insurance policy against personal injury, but something which, like air and food, is necessary for well-being and fulfilment. This in itself does not constitute a theory. It is a presupposition, a premise upon which differing bodies of theory might be built. It is possible, therefore, to identify many other theorists besides Aristotle who share or inherit this outlook. Among them we may mention Aquinas, Grotius, Montesquieu, Hegel, and the British philosophers Bosanquet and T.H. Green. This outlook tends to be associated, in its different forms, with two kinds of social and political theory in particular. These are Natural Law theory (as in Aquinas, Grotius, and Montesquieu) and the "organic" theory of the state (as in Hegel, Bosanquet, and Green). I call this the Aristotelian tradition.

Running alongside the Aristotelian tradition for most of its history there is another approach, which might be labeled the Augustinian tradition. St. Augustine of Hippo, in his famous work *The City of God*, describes the earthly state as entirely factitious; a result of the wickedness of fallen human nature, usually oppressive, never more than a

necessary evil, and only worthy of our submission insofar as it may
protect us from worse oppression still. "Nature" here takes on a somewhat different aspect, concerned not primarily with the need of man for
the state as a prerequisite of self-fulfilment, but with the instinct of
self-preservation. Submission to political authority is not a matter of
seeking to participate in a quest for collective well-being, but of staving
off destruction and death. There is benefit in it, but it is grudgingly
conceded: ". . . it would be incorrect to say that the goods which this
city desires are not goods, since even that city is better, in its own
human way, by their possession."[4] In the Augustinian tradition the
state is chiefly an imposition on humanity, restricting human nature in
its freedom rather than enabling it to fulfil itself. I can cite a number of
well-known thinkers who have adopted this type of view, such as
Marsilius, Machiavelli, Luther, Hooker, Hobbes, Locke, and most of the
Social Contract school — Spinoza, Tom Paine, Bentham, Proudhon,
Marx, and many modern writers, notably Robert Nozick. It would be
wrong to see these writers as representing any one specific theory about
the state; I am attempting merely to draw attention to this one feature
which they all have in common — that of regarding the state as artificial,
as a human artifact, and as essentially restrictive. Some of them, such as
Hooker, Hobbes, and Locke, conclude from these assumptions that
some kind of fictitious device (the original "Social Contract") must be
introduced to explain the state's claim on us, while others, such as
Luther, Proudhon, and Marx, have drawn the conclusion that the state
itself is, or ought to be, redundant in the long run.

In some periods of history the Aristotelian view of the state has
tended to prevail, while in others the main current of thought has run
along Augustinian lines. I want to suggest here that the present-day
climate of political thought is overwhelmingly Augustinian in its bias.
Notice that the logic of the two positions differs in the following way.
While the Aristotelian is committed to the view that some form of
political organization is natural to man, the Augustinian must consider
that all such forms are unnatural. Yet not all those whose outlook might
be labeled Augustinian agree on the way in which this is the case.
Broadly speaking, we may identify two divergent tendencies. The
characteristic feature of the Augustinian outlook is that of seeing the
state as something imposed artificially, and this might be expressed
loosely as saying that authority is seen as a necessary evil. But this is not
quite accurate. For some believe the state to be necessary though not
exactly an evil, while others believe it to be an evil which is not

necessary! All of them, in other words, tend to stress the one aspect at the expense of the other. Thus we have two rather different pictures of the state from within the Augustinian tradition. Once again neither constitutes a well-defined theory, and, partly for this reason and partly because I want to recommend a degree of skepticism concerning both of them, I shall call them "myths."

The first I shall refer to as the Myth of the Fortress. This is the idea of the state as having primarily a protective function. On this view the state is an artifice which, like a medieval castle, keeps us safe by erecting walls around us. The walls are not to prevent us from getting outside, though it would be foolish and dangerous to try to do so. They exist rather to keep at bay chaos, anarchy, uncertainty, arbitrary violence and aggression, and all those facets of human nature which cannot be brought inside the pale of civilized society. This picture is probably best exemplified in the case of the seventeenth-century writer Thomas Hobbes. However bad the state may be, for Hobbes, it is always preferable to the State of Nature, the original condition of humanity in the absence of political authority. People accept it for the purpose of "getting themselves out from that miserable condition of war, which is necessarily consequent . . . to the natural passions of men, when there is no visible power to keep them in awe." Here is the complete antithesis of the Aristotelian view. It is Nature itself which is kept at bay by the structure we erect. The same theme is echoed in the eighteenth century by David Hume when he says, "Our primary instincts lead us either to indulge ourselves in unlimited freedom, or to seek dominion over others; and it is reflection only which engages us to sacrifice such strong passions to the interests of peace and public order." It has also its modern adherents, the chief of whom is probably the American philosopher Robert Nozick. He analyzes the origin of the state in terms of "protective associations." These, according to Nozick, are to be seen as responses to the threat of a State of Nature:

> In a state of nature an individual may himself enforce his rights, defend himself, and punish. . . . Others may join with him in his defence, at his call. They may join with him to repulse an attacker or go after an aggressor because they are public spirited, or because they are his friends, or because he has helped them in the past, or because they wish him to help them in future, or in exchange for something.[5]

Nozick does entertain the possibility of pure public-spiritedness or disinterested friendship as motives, and he is not committed to the depressing psychological egoism of Hobbes. Yet his picture is still overwhelmingly pessimistic. There is no suggestion that the state might exist at least partly in order to help people express their own, social, nature. The Myth of the Fortress, in all its forms, paints a gloomy picture of the state's function, little less gloomy than its picture of the condition of the individual without it. It is a picture of people clinging together in organized groups not because they find it congenial to live together in this way, but simply out of fear of being cast into the outer darkness of the State of Nature. Since we do not know what it is like to live without any form of political authority, this fear is to some extent a superstitious one. However, we do know enough about what happens when the system of law and order breaks down — in riot, in civil war, in slums and urban "no-go areas," to understand where the attraction lies in the idea of the state as fortress.

The Myth of the Prison rests on similar Augustinian premises regarding the basic artificiality of the state. It is, according to this myth, an edifice which has been consciously created, but this time not for protection, even from ourselves, but for restraint. It is not a fortress which protects its inmates, but a prison designed to keep them in a condition of servitude. The walls are there not for our own good, but to keep us in, and it would be in our own best interests to demolish them and let in not the chaos, but the fresh air. Whereas the fortress was a small area of light and security in a landscape of darkness and danger, the prison is the opposite. Inside, all is dullness and misery, while outside the walls are the sunlight and freedom which we are prevented from enjoying. Perhaps the best-known statement of this view is Proudhon's:

> To be governed is to be watched, inspected, spied upon, law-driven, numbered, regulated, enrolled, indoctrinated, preached at, controlled, checked, estimated, valued, censured, commanded, by creatures who have neither the right nor the wisdom nor the virtue to do so. To be governed is to be at every operation, at every transaction noted, registered, counted, taxed, stamped, measured, numbered, assessed, licensed, authorized, admonished, prevented, forbidden, reformed, corrected, punished. It is, under pretext of public utility, and in the name of the general interest, to be placed under contribution, drilled, fleeced, exploited, monopolised, extorted from, squeezed, hoaxed, robbed; then, at the slightest resistance, the first word of complaint, to be repressed, vilified, harassed, hunted down, abused, clubbed, disarmed, bound, choked, imprisoned, judged, condemned, sold, betrayed; and to crown all, mocked, ridiculed, derided, outraged, dishonoured. That is government. . . .[6]

This point of view has its interest, for it possesses much the same ring as a great deal that has been written about the potential threats of information technology. Had Proudhon come face to face with the modern data bank, there is not much doubt what he would have thought of it. Yet for most of us the picture he paints is not true to life even as regards the present, let alone the future. If this is what it is to be governed, what, we may wonder, is it like to be *mis*governed? The answer is that for such writers the distinction does not exist — there is only misgovernment, and every strengthening of the state's power to keep a check on us is another step toward further misgovernment. This view also has many echoes in other influential thinkers (though perhaps not all quite so vociferous). Marx saw political power as essentially the oppression of one class by another, and it is a short step from this to the idea that ideally the state will "wither away." Engels, writing after Marx's death, commits himself further, saying: "As soon as there is no longer any social class to be held in subjection . . . nothing more remains to be repressed, and a special repressive force, a state, is no longer necessary. . . . The state is not 'abolished'. It dies out."

This kind of theory has an obvious appeal for those who at present live under a manifestly oppressive government or regime. But it is an easy step from blaming oppression on the Government to blaming it on government in general. Hence the nineteenth-century American writer Henry David Thoreau:

> I heartily accept the motto — "That government is best which governs least;" and I should like to see it acted up to more rapidly and systematically. Carried out, it finally amounts to this, which I also believe — "That government is best which governs not at all;" and when men are prepared for it, that will be the kind of government which they will have.[7]

The prison myth acquires plausibility partly by invoking somewhat untypical images. Some states might be like prisons — many are not. If we lived in a society in which there was so much plenty (and such writers as Marx seem to have made this assumption) and so little divergence of interests that no one had a motive for lawlessness, the state might present itself as a pointless bundle of restrictions. But we do not.

One reason for spending some time on the discussion of these "myths" is precisely that they *are* myths in the above sense. This need not necessarily mean that they contain nothing which is true. Some societies lean toward the Fortress image, and some toward that of the Prison. Neither, however, is likely to be the whole truth. What we have is, as it were, pictures of the fundamental nature of the state and its organization. For this reason they are often more use to a person attempting to explain the genesis of certain attitudes toward the state's authority than they are to those who actually espouse them. In this respect they throw light on what, in the last chapter, I called the cultural factor. I have a strong suspicion that these myths belong not only to respective schools of political theory, but also (and perhaps predominantly) to those who occupy different positions within a society. To the governed, who do not participate to any great extent in the framing of policy, and who are often unaware of the wider issues of political philosophy, the state may indeed be liable to present itself as largely a bundle of pointless restrictions and regulations. The Myth of the Prison holds an obvious attraction for many people, and it is inevitable that they will view the application of new technology in the service of the state as little more than a set of devices for tightening those restrictions and enforcing those pointless regulations. On the other hand, those actively concerned in the business of government can sometimes be excused if their view of things is colored rather by the Myth of the Fortress. National security, both civil and international, is their concern, and there is no mystery about why they will tend to look on any means, especially means as powerful as are now available, for strengthening their hand in this respect, as not only harmless but a positive asset. It is true that national security is not the only responsibility of government, and there are ways in which information technology can be used to further such aims as freedom and democracy as well as law, order, and defense (the possibilities which it creates for the wider availability of information have an obvious role to play). Here, however, we are concerned only with the potential of such technology as a force for repression and surveillance. Again it must be emphasized that if these are likely to become the chief uses to which it is put, the blame cannot be on the technology itself. Some politically unhealthy situation must already obtain before such an unbalanced exploitation of it can be a serious option. Only in an unhealthy political climate can national security be made out to take precedence over the liberty, dignity, and privacy of its people. This is not to say that such an unhealthy state of affairs does not exist in many societies with which we are familiar. The point made here is that the fault does not lie essentially in the technological capability as such, for the question "Capability for what?" is not one to which the technology itself contains an answer.

Authoritarianism and Accountability

None of this means that the sort of information technology we are discussing is going to lack negative effects on political freedom or civil liberties. As I have already emphasized, a future threat never conforms to the pattern of past ones. What might such a genuine threat be like? The novelty of a new threat only limits our ability to rely on induction from past cases: it does not prevent us from keeping our eyes open and making well-informed predictions based on extrapolation from present trends. Indeed we are bound to do this.

Having expressed some skepticism concerning the idea of a dramatic rise of totalitarianism or the like, I may regard the more credible scenario (though it is hard to make any judgment about just how likely it is) to be a gradual encroachment of information technology on the lives of citizens in such a way that certain kinds of deviation become more easily detectable and certain kinds of laws perhaps easier to enforce. I say certain kinds, for the effect of computerization would be unlikely to consist in a uniform enhancement of the state's ability to detect all crimes and to enforce all laws. Rather, those "offenses" against the state which form part of a pattern of character and behavior manifesting itself over long periods of time, for example, in public actions and membership of organizations, may be expected to be the *forte* of computerized enforcement. Thus technology may help very little to prevent and detect murders, for example, but will probably be very useful to keep check on leaders of protest movements and instigators of civil disobedience (besides, of course, a lot of other, more obviously wicked, activities like terrorism and organized crime).

The kind of situation I am now envisaging does not, then, involve a radical break with existing political systems and authority structures, but is continuous with them, differing only in the degree of what would commonly be called authoritarianism. This concept is perhaps even harder to grasp than some of those discussed farther back. It cannot simply mean that the state is efficient at enforcing its laws: if it meant this, everyone would be in favor of authoritarianism. Nor can it mean merely that the penalties for breaking laws are stiff ones, for then the only people to feel the weight of it would be convicted lawbreakers. It has more to do with the number and kind of things which are illegal. A state in which the law casts a wide net, making illegal a very broad range of activities, is an authoritairan state. And this is the case to an even greater extent where the illegal activities include, for instance, the holding of certain opinions or the advocating of particular policies. Authoritarianism is the trend of which totalitarianism is the limiting case. It need not necessarily involve radical constitutional changes, one-party government, or even complete control of the channels of communication and propaganda. Authoritarianism can engrain itself in a tradition or political climate in such a way that it is capable of surviving changes of government — the differences between the specific policies of different parties becoming less significant the more it gains a hold. It can arise in a creeping and insidious fashion far removed from the cataclysmic revolution of Orwell's state or the apocalyptic vision of popular futurology. Just for this reason it holds a special danger.

Furthermore, because it is gradual and does not involve the kind of upheaval which requires an independent motive, and because of the sort of activities which computers are good at keeping a check on, it is precisely the sort of trend which could be fuelled by the computerization of government. Among other things, to make illegal the kinds of activity which we are good at detecting, to tailor our laws to what we are good at enforcing, is a line of least resistance which can prove very tempting. (It is easier to lock up suspects than to prevent free men from committing crimes, more convenient to ban political demonstrations than to keep the peace when they occur.) And there is some evidence, including facts such as those cited near the beginning of this chapter, to suggest that this is the sort of thing which is already happening in many technologically advanced societies.

The reason is not far to seek, and is an aspect of what I referred to in the last chapter as the human factor. I do not need to posit any actual malice or extraordinary lust for power on the part of the users in order to explain why this particular scenario is a credible one. All I need to assume is the existence of a government or governing class composed of fallible, vulnerable human beings with the ordinary kinds of motivations — remaining in office, doing the best for their party and their country, trying to control crime, impressing their colleagues, and so on. Add to this the temptation to take a line of least resistance, to opt for what is possible and easily available rather than what is really appropriate though difficult to attain, and it is not difficult to see how the slide into authoritarianism can occur without anyone necessarily actively desiring it.

If this, unlike some of the projections discussed above, is a real and immediate threat, what can be done about it? Part of the answer to this question is that, once it has been allowed to run its course to a certain point, it is possible that very little at all can be done. This is one of the genuine causes for alarm regarding the technologization of government. So long as the hardware is with us, its effects may be irreversible. Technology is not going to put anyone in power, but it may be going to keep them there, in a way which goes beyond the potential of any techniques known previously for the perpetuation of power. From this point of view it does not much matter who the "them" are.

In order to prevent this situation from coming about, it is necessary to ensure at least two things. The first is that government is properly accountable to the governed, to control carefully the ability of the administration to take independent decisions which affect the development of our society. This does not just mean holding periodic elections, which, although desirable on more general grounds, are notoriously ineffective as a means of seeing to it that politicians do as we wish them to do.

This brings me to the second requirement. In order to make accountability work, it is necessary that the population be adequately informed. One thing which has emerged from this chapter is that lack of understanding is probably the chief obstacle to the public's ability to come to terms with new technology and to steer its use in the direction they desire, rather than being constrained to follow blindly the guidance of "experts."

These are not requirements which gain their value only incidentally as a result of the situation caused by computerization. They are not *ad hoc* solutions. Rather, they are long-standing goals of the democratic tradition. The contribution of the technological revolution has not been to create the need for these things to be regarded as valuable (see the discussion in chapter 1, of creating new values versus finding new ways of implementing old ones), but to enhance their importance and to make their cause more urgent. These themes of the need for accountability and the corresponding need for an informed public will be taken up again, especially in the last chapter, in connection with at least one other accompanying theme which has not yet been discussed.

4. To Err Is Human

Some years ago a fairly ordinary family was surprised when a mail van drew up outside their house and, instead of the usual half-dozen or so letters, delivered several sacks full of mail to the door. These turned out to contain many hundred identical copies of a magazine to which one of the family happened to subscribe. What had happened was that a computer, supposedly programmed to print the names and addresses of subscribers on the envelopes, had printed the same name and address (the first on the list) on every envelope! This is only one of many instances which could be cited in support of the view that computerized systems are particularly liable to errors which inconvenience (at best) those who are on the receiving end. Most examples are neither so amusing nor so harmless. They include stories of data about one person (including a criminal record) being confused with data on a different person of the same surname; sums of money being multiplied or divided by factors of ten, a hundred, or a thousand; and out-of-date computer records leading to a rehabilitated person's being refused a job on grounds of mental illness.[1] Before going on to discuss the reasonableness of fears arising from such instances, let me briefly review the question in relation to the subject of the last chapter.

A Clash of Attitudes

There is on first sight a curiously paradoxical feature of many people's attitudes to information technology. On the one hand, it is seen as sinister, threatening, and likely in the end to result in repression and terror; on the other hand, it is seen as making for inefficiency, incompetence, error, and waste of time and resources. The installation of a computer in an organization is frequently ridiculed as little more than an excuse for the shortcomings of the organization's staff (and sometimes, as we shall see, it is little more than that). But surely we cannot have it both ways. Computer technology cannot at the same time be both a deadly threat to our freedom, an irresistible weapon in the hands of our political masters, and also a kind of confidence trick, superficially flashy and impressive yet essentially clumsy and inefficient. What sense can we make of this?

First, not all of the wisecracks about the absurdity of computerization should be taken seriously or at face value (and not all that is unserious is necessarily frivolous). Some humor is a case of whistling in the dark, for we are always inclined to make a joke at the expense of that which worries or frightens us. How could Hitler have been both a ridiculous, laughable little man and also a threat to the peace and freedom of the world? Yet few people had much difficulty in combining the two attitudes at the time.

Secondly, there is both a truth and a falsehood contained in this paradoxical conflict of attitudes. The truth is that such technology is capable both of creating a havoc worse than that of any system it may have superseded and also of being used in a way which is menacingly efficient. The falsehood lies in supposing that it must be essentially the one thing or the other. I argued in chapter 2 that information technology is at bottom neutral with respect to the range of possible applications it allows, the "bias," if any, being added by human nature or by conscious human decision. And this is true of the computer's tendency to make, or not to make, errors of a certain kind. But it is true in a different way, and for an even stronger reason.

Whose Mistakes?

Computers do not make mistakes. Nor does this mean that they are infallible. It is a result of the fact that only something which possesses a conception of what it is attempting to do — which has an idea of what it would be to do the thing correctly — can properly be said to make a mistake. A computer is not *trying* to do anything at all. It simply does whatever it in fact does, and we as the users make use of it for purposes which are our purposes. Computers are neither stupid nor bright. They neither make mistakes nor get things right. (This is true in the same way that it is true that a machine like a bear-trap cannot get something right or wrong: it springs too early or too late, or doesn't spring at all, but it is only right or wrong relative to *our* intentions for it.)

The only way to avoid this particular conclusion would be to accept that these machines have a mental life, in the sense that they can follow certain rules with a certain purpose "in mind," i.e., that they have a real conception of the task that they are engaged in. This would bring it about that they could be said to be mistaken (as opposed to merely containing the wrong bit of data), to be attentive (rather than simply operating below their full potential), or to be fallible (instead of just doing something other than what we want them to do). The important thing to bear in mind here is that most experts are agreed that, even if it is possible in principle for computers to have genuine intelligence ("intentionality"), the sorts of machines which we are talking about here do not. It is just possible that at some time in the future machines may be properly said in a non-metaphorical sense to think, intend, know, guess, or make correct or incorrect judgments. What is not the least bit plausible is that the everyday computer used for regular information storage has any of these capacities at all. The argument for machine intelligence in general rests on the idea of consciousness as something which "emerges" at a certain level of complexity and sophistication. To credit the computer in the local store with this degree of sophistication would be a *reductio ad absurdum* of the whole idea.

Genuine error, when it occurs, is an error on the part of human beings. It may be an error in what is put into a computer, or in the *way* it is put in. It may be a mistake in reading or interpreting what comes out of the machine, or "interrogating" in an inept way. On the other hand, it may be due to a fault in the way the computer has been programmed, which is simply a human fault one step removed, for the fault will lie with the person who originally wrote the program. Again, it may be the machine itself which is faulty — for there may be a loose connection, or some "noise" (unwanted electrical impulses which are not genuine signals) on the lines. But this would not be a mistake on the computer's part, any more than having an attack of measles is a mistake on the part of a human being.

All the talk we hear about computer errors and so on has a tendency to blind us to the fact that, in the last analysis, it is we as human beings who make the mistakes. It also tends to prevent us from seeing the grain of truth in the fears engendered by examples such as that cited at the beginning of this chapter. The grain of truth lies in the fact that machines of the sort which we possess today tend not to create but to magnify errors. Precisely because the machine has no intelligence in any literal sense, it is unable to exercise the kind of open-ended control which a human being can. Tell a computer to print the same name on six thousand envelopes, and it will not think there is anything even the slightest bit odd about the request — for it will not think anything about it at all, it will just do it. And it will do it so quickly and thoroughly that the whole job is likely to be completed without anybody capable of making a judgment about it having either the need or perhaps even the opportunity to intervene. It is this magnification of human error and the out-of-sight quality of the machine's operation which are the real causes for worry.

And yet this kind of worry is in itself fairly trivial. It is at least a simple matter of means and ends: nobody wants these absurdities to occur, and the only question left is how to prevent them. Unless we think that they are in principle ineradicable once we accept the computerization of information, there is certainly no ethical problem connection with them — they are simply a nuisance to be got rid of. It may be that machine errors are in principle ineradicable, though I cannot think what an argument to this effect would even look like. It would still remain another question as to what should be done as a result. For not only do computers tend to magnify errors, they also magnify our capacity for doing things correctly, and, although some computer users would be tempted to disagree, they do run properly most of the time. The magnification of human error is hardly a reason for thinking this kind of technology is a bad thing in general, and so the only course open to us is to try and improve it — which conclusion hardly represents a striking breakthrough in moral philosophy! In fact, the interesting moral aspect of this issue lies not here, but close at hand.

Passing the Buck

The most significant fact about computers in relation to error, apart from their magnification of human mistakes, is their apparent capacity for *excusing* the mistakes of human beings. Nearly everyone must be familiar with the experience of having cause to complain of the shortcoming of some organization and being told, "The computer made a mistake," or "It's the computer — it still thinks it's yesterday." There should be no further need to labor the point that such statements must be either lies, metaphors, or mistakes. The significant thing to notice is the way in which the buck has been passed. I say "the way in which" rather than "the fact that" with good reason. For this sort of response depends precisely on exploiting the ambiguity between the real sense in which a person, such as the manager, might have made a mistake, or might think it is still yesterday, and the metaphorical sense in which the same thing may be said of a machine. Given what has emerged in the last section, it should be clear that if there has indeed been a mistake, it is somebody's mistake and that this somebody cannot be the machine. We do blame the implements we use for some unsatisfactory results: "I'm sorry the table wobbles, but the screwdriver was bent." But there is a difference between blaming a person and blaming a tool. Tools (including machines) can certainly be faulty, but they cannot be at fault in the way that people can. The fault is a different sort of fault, depending on whether it is that of the manufacturer or is an "act of God" (the screwdriver is bent because it was made bent or because it was trodden on by a horse; the computer overheats because the wrong kind of solder was used or because of a heatwave). In either case the buck cannot possibly stop with the machine itself: it stops either with natural forces or with the person who made or who programmed the machine. The difference between the workman who blames his tools and the workman who blames the tool-maker is a real one, but it is nowhere more ignored and systematically blurred than in people's dealings with electronic machinery.

Sometimes, of course, it is natural that the locus of blame should simply disappear to a vanishing point for all practical purposes. When my colleague says, "I can't read your handwriting," and I reply, "It's this damn pen — it won't write straight," we do not bother to pursue the question of who made the pen and what should be done to bring that person to account. But buying a ballpoint pen for one's use and installing a computer system for purposes which affect the general public in significant ways are two different things. It is in the latter sort of case that the real trouble arises.

Screwdrivers are the kinds of things which most people understand reasonably well. Even if we have not worked out the physical theory of how and why they operate, we at least know that they work in particular ways, and roughly the type of thing that can go wrong with them. Computers are different. They are, to many people, much like an alien form of life (and the life aspect plays no small part in many of the misunderstandings). When we are told that the machine thinks it is Tuesday, we are inclined to take the matter no farther. If we do take it farther, we might be informed, if we are very lucky, that the software has not been made properly compatible with the hardware, that the program is looping where it should not be, or that there is a bug in the assembler. Unless we are very brave indeed, we will certainly take the matter no further than this. We come to a very definite dead end. The buck has been passed not to another person, of whom we could inquire just what he thinks he is playing at, but to something which is non-human (or subhuman, or superhuman). This is one reason for the feeling of dehumanization in our relationships with our modern social environment, which I shall say more about in chapter 7.

Paradoxically there is at least one kind of ethical argument which militates against our having too much to do with the machines which keep the records on us. If we are allowed to have contact with the machine itself, problems of security are prone to arise vis-à-vis other people whose records are kept alongside our own. Access to the records by individual clients can be dangerous as well as beneficial from a human rights point of view, and much has been made of this in some circles.

But there is an aspect of ignorance about computers and detachment from their actual operation which lies even deeper. This is ignorance on the part of the very people who own, install, and operate them. When it comes to hammers, screwdrivers, and other familiar and simple bits of machinery there is a general understanding of the conditions under which someone ought to have known better than to do the job with those tools, and the conditions under which he cannot really be held responsible. Lack of education in information technology *on the side* of the users themselves creates a situation in which this kind of understanding does not exist, and in which accountability is very hard to ascribe. This brings me to an issue which must now be addressed.

The Goal of Computer Literacy

Every so often it happens that a new educational disease is diagnosed, from which nearly everyone is found to be suffering. Innumeracy in the arts subjects followed hard on the heels of illiteracy among scientists. "Irrelevance," by which most subjects were once discovered to be infected in the form of irrelevance to modern society, is now being resurrected in certain areas as irrelevance to economic performance. But surely the most successful piece of diagnosis in recent years has been the discovery that most people are "computer illiterate." Like Monsieur Jourdain and his prose-speaking, they probably never knew it.

What is this capability which nearly everybody lacks? The trouble is that the computer literati themselves are not agreed on a suitable characterization, despite a great deal of deliberation — which is embarrassing from the point of view of being able to tell when the patient is cured.[2] Nevertheless, it is possible to get some idea of what is meant by considering the very wide range of things which would count as symptoms of computer *illiteracy*. Examples of the different kinds, or grades, of symptom might be as follows:

(i) being unable to identify or correct an error in a computer used in one's job,

(ii) being unable to program a computer,

(iii) failing to understand the rudiments of any computer language,

(iv) lacking competence in selecting a computer to install for a particular purpose,

(v) being unable to operate a computer at an elementary level (inserting disks the wrong way up, etc.),

(vi) being unable to understand things written *by* (as opposed to *for*) a computer, and

(vii) staring vacantly at the bar ceiling when friends and colleagues discuss the relative merits of their micros.

It is often hard to resist the suspicion that it is (vii) which is meant to be the most worrying symptom of all. Nevertheless, each of these types or shades of inability tells us something.

What is highly questionable, however, is whether all these different things hang together in such a way as to yield a single concept of what it is to be computer literate. The kinds of skills indicated by the above list can perhaps be seen as falling into three categories, in descending order of technicality:

(a) hardware and programming skills (actually very different, but assimilable for our purposes here)

(b) end-user skills (ability to use a computer, given that it is already in good order and properly programmed)

(c) social skills connected with computers (ability to read computer-written material without assistance, knowledge of jargon, general background knowledge).

Category (a) would seem to go far beyond what is required in order to be regarded as merely literate. Knowledge of computer hardware is a very specialized business, and a closed book even to many who work professionally with computers. Programming is itself a professional skill, though it is possible even for children to pick up a working knowledge of how to write simple programs in an elementary language such as BASIC. The trouble with regarding this very cursory acquaintance with programming as a useful ability has two sides to it. First, it is an ability for which little genuine use would be found by anyone not intending to take up programming either as a career or as a very serious hobby. There is no real demand for third-rate programming: all viable commercial applications of computers (and most leisure ones as well) have packages put together by professional programmers. Secondly, one cannot simply "learn to program" computers — what one learns is how to handle a particular programming *language*. The result of having no genuine use for one's knowledge of a given language is that one forgets it very quickly. It is not like the ability to swim or ride a bicycle which, once internalized, is never lost however long it lies unused, but more like the ability to play a particular piece of music or to remember semaphore or Morse code, activities that need hands-on practice. There is perhaps a grain of truth in the idea that it might be useful to teach a little about programming as a part of general computer literacy. This lies in the fact that a little acquaintance with a few different programming languages will tend to leave a person with a greater facility for picking up any given language of one of the standard kinds in the future — but whether he or she will actually need that facility remains another matter.

Category (c) appears to be in the opposite position. Someone whose only knowledge of computers lies in the ability to read printouts, to manipulate the jargon of the subject, and to regale friends with bits of general knowledge of the type found in popular computing magazines cannot truly be said to possess an ability with computers at all. What such a person has may better be described as the semblance or illusion of an ability. In many ways there is no harm in this, and I certainly do not wish to suggest that general knowledge of any kind is a bad thing. Where it can do harm, however (and this has an important bearing on what was said in the last section), is in the ease with which a person possessing a very small smattering of knowledge of this kind is often able to "blind with science" a person without even a spurious knowledge. One can detect a danger of such very elementary knowledge becoming part of the required stock-in-trade of workers in lower and middle management, as a very effective means of buck-passing. And it would not perhaps be going too far to say that this is what is already happening.

As might now be expected, it is category (b) which I would wish to point to as containing the genuinely useful skills for someone whose job involves working with computers at all closely. Here the problem is different once again. Like the "social" skills, end-user skills are not difficult to learn at the level at which they would be required by most users; but like programming skills they are specialized. That is, there is no way of simply teaching someone to use a computer terminal, any more than someone can be simply taught to use, say, an electric motor.

It depends entirely on what kind of machine it is, what it is being used for, what role in the entire system that person is being called upon to play, and so on. This is why, in the end, I want to argue that computer literacy, conceived as a single set of skills which is nevertheless generally useful, is a somewhat misguided goal. What is required is not the inculcation, into a whole generation of people, of a single body of knowledge and ability, but a clear and thorough understanding, on the part of persons who are called on to act as mediators between the computer and the general public, of those particular aspects which are relevant to their own professional responsibilities.

Accountability Again

To recapitulate a little, I pointed in the last section but one to two reasons why human error is important in connection with the ethics of information technology. The first was that computerization makes it more simple than ever to pass the blame on until it reaches something which cannot usefully be blamed. The second, connected reason was that ignorance can provide a useful, and quite often a justified, defense against blame. Part of the reason for the feeling of hopelessness and futility which one experiences in trying to trace the buck which is being passed springs from the fact that those whose function it ought to be to mediate between the client and the computerized "system" do not possess sufficient understanding of the latter to be held properly accountable. This occurs both in public bodies and in private corporations; it is not characteristic of just one kind of agency or organization but permeates our society. Nor is it restricted to any one level within such organizations, but tends to manifest itself in different ways throughout the administrative hierarchy. I further argued in the last section that the remedy for this cannot lie in some broad, shallow concept such as computer literacy for all, but rather in a thorough and specific education in those aspects of this immensely wide subject which are relevant to the use which a particular person needs to make of it.

What is also required, however, is a certain standard of education and "informed-ness" on the part of those on the receiving end of the technology. This is distinct from the notion of computer literacy, on which I hope I have shed some justified doubt. The capacity to remain unhoodwinked by spurious explanations, to be immune to blinding-by-science, is not a matter of understanding what the experts understand, or even acquiring a smattering of it, so much as the exercising of a robust common sense which tends to go along with a certain general level of education and awareness. In a world of specialists and specializations, what is needed is not a desperate attempt to keep up with everything, but a level-headed confidence in the face of that which we do not fully understand. This is, perhaps, a different sort of literacy, and a sort which we badly lack at the moment.

Finally, we should expect a certain openness on the part of the computer literati themselves; a genuine desire to be understood rather than merely admired. It is very easy for somebody else's specialization to seem much more mystifying and impenetrable than it really is, and this goes for computers as much as anything else. The problems of explaining what is actually going on to someone without a specialized knowledge are not really as great as they are often made to seem. If the will to do this is largely missing, it is perhaps time we began insisting on it more. We cannot afford to become a society with two cultures.

All of this connects with the arguments raised toward the end of the last chapter regarding the importance of an educated public, ensuring an acceptable level of public participation in decision-making, and avoiding a widening of the gulf between those on the inside and those on the outside of the computerized bureaucracy around us. Time and time again, as we view our subject from different angles, we will find the argument for these complementary principles of an accountable administration and an educated public.

5. Private Lives

In the last two chapters I discussed two of the major worries regarding the large-scale storage of personal data, and I looked at some of the main ethical issues surrounding these areas of concern. I now want to suggest a third area as deserving of attention: privacy. This issue has connections with those already covered: totalitarianism is necessarily destructive of privacy, and the unintentional misuse of information (or the use of misinformation) can easily have such effects. However, I have tried to keep the question of privacy separate, since it is important in its own right, and its distinctness needs stressing. Privacy is not merely a matter of not living under a tyranny, nor simply of ensuring that all information collected about us is accurate. Threats to privacy can arise in democracies as well as in dictatorships, in well-run societies besides inefficient ones.

The initial difficulty (and perhaps even the greatest) in talking about privacy is that of formulating a working definition of the concept. While the other sources of anxiety we have seen are fairly easily identifiable, the threat to privacy is not, or not always. One reason is that the notion of privacy is itself unclear. Although the word privacy is one which we all know how to use more or less correctly, when we try to pin down just what we mean by it, even in a given context, it has a tendency to elude us.

Fortunately it is not necessary to go into detail here concerning privacy in general, but only chiefly as it relates to the holding of information about us. Nevertheless, it is inevitable that some light must be shed on the broader concept.

Privacy and Information

There is good reason to believe that privacy, in one form or another, is among what we may regard as basic human needs, and, therefore, arguably, human rights. If we are to go beyond the mere necessities of biological survival and allow some deep-rooted and universal instincts constitutive of human needs, some opportunity for privacy (in a sense which is yet to be clarified) must surely be among these. A striking indication of this is provided by the fact that which particular areas of life are regarded as appropriate objects of privacy is something that varies quite widely from one society to another, but that the existence of some such areas is universal.

This being so, it may be asked why we should become especially alarmed that a particular change is taking place in the pattern of privacy expectations at the present time — namely that information about people is becoming more available, more easily, and in larger quantities, than ever before. After all, changes in the pattern have occurred in the past. It may be pointed out, for example, that death tended to be a more public event in the last century than it is today, but that sex was then on the whole a more private activity than it now is. We are living through yet another change in the pattern. Is it only lack of historical sense which prevents us from accepting it unhesitatingly?

The answer to this must be no. The privacy of knowledge and information cannot easily be placed on the same footing as the privacy of certain situations, events, and activities such as sex, death, buying and selling, eating and sleeping, and so on. Information by its nature refers outside itself: it is about something. And what it may be about includes any of these other areas of life. The issue of the privacy of information is, therefore, a second-order issue. This is yet another reason for thinking that we are not just dealing essentially with an old problem in a new guise.

With this in mind let me move toward a rough definition of privacy in this sort of context. To begin with I would like to draw attention to a transition which I believe has occurred in attitudes, especially "official" attitudes, concerning privacy in recent decades.

Changing Emphasis in the Privacy Argument

Writing about the legal aspect of privacy in 1960, the American jurist Dean Prosser identified four elements which he claimed were present in the traditional idea of the right to privacy as he believed it to be embodied in United States law. These were:

(1) protection against intrusion on one's seclusion or private affairs,
(2) prevention of the disclosure of embarrassing facts,
(3) protection against being placed in a false light, and
(4) defense against the appropriation of one's name or likeness for commercial purposes.[1]

It is significant that none of these elements, nor all of them taken together, seems to answer to what we might ordinarily mean by privacy today.

It is not, for instance, that we object to just *any* intrusion on our private affairs. Most people would now agree that there is hardly any area of our lives about which someone might not at some time have just cause to inquire. The question is then one of what constitutes a just cause, and which sorts of intrusions are to count as unwarranted. Prosser speaks of the disclosure of "embarrassing" facts. But the facts need not always be embarrassing for their disclosure to count as an unwarranted breach of privacy — I might as easily be annoyed at someone's systematically collecting information about my (supposedly discreet) charitable activities as about my sex life. Conversely there may be embarrassing facts about a person which he has no right to regard as private. Nor (and this will be seen to be especially relevant to today's situation) need it be the disclosure of such facts which is the crux of my objection, for we are often more concerned at what might be stored in secret files and data banks than about what is made public. It may be that it is always at least the threat of disclosure, even if only to certain people, which is the reason for objecting to such storage; however, it is not entirely clear that this must be the case, and even if it is we tend to feel with good reason that our privacy has been violated as soon as the information is thus collected and stored, and not just after it has been disclosed. Moving on to Prosser's third point, it is not normally thought necessary for a breach of privacy that someone is displayed in a false light — I can sometimes justifiably protest against being displayed at all (false lights have more to do with defamation than with breach of privacy). And the final element in Prosser's analysis surely does not apply to most of us at all — indeed we might be very gratified if it did!

This (perhaps somewhat dated) approach to privacy is, I would suggest, almost the very reverse of that embodied in current thinking, both popular and sophisticated. The picture presented in Prosser's account is that of a public figure attempting to defend his or her personal life against intrusion by the curious man in the street, as represented by the newspaper reporter or the advertising copy-writer. The picture which frightens most of us at present is rather that of the man in the street attempting to guard his personal life against intrusion by the curious public figure, as represented by the police, the government agency, or the credit company. This is one way in which not only the objects of privacy, but the kind of privacy in question (the "point" of it, as one might say) has changed with time and circumstances. It is a change which has been brought about largely by new techniques in the technology of information.

Privacy as Secrecy

Continuing the attempt to characterize what is designated by privacy in connection with information, I shall mention a few things which it is not. There are two good reasons for this somewhat seemingly negative approach. The first is that definition by process of elimination can (as Plato clearly knew) be very fruitful. The second, and more important, is that I would like to establish the independence and irreducibility of the concept of privacy. I wish, that is, to avoid the kind of definition which is sometimes called "nothing-buttery," in which a speaker or writer tries to minimize the importance of something by showing that it is "nothing but" something else. After that I shall give a more positive account of privacy vis-à-vis information, and draw some important implications from it with regard to the present technological situation. In this section I shall point to some differences between privacy and secrecy.

Privacy of information clearly has something to do with the withholding of information from someone. It is tempting to think that if some fact or body of facts is deliberately withheld, it must be a secret, and that privacy in this respect therefore is, or at least essentially involves, a form of secrecy. This identification is, however, mistaken. The withholding of information can be either an active or a passive gesture. If we take positive steps to conceal information, it is natural to call this information secret and to refer to the concealment as "keeping a secret." But it is also possible to withhold information in the sense that one simply does not volunteer it, though one might disclose the facts in question if actually requested to do so. Thus I withhold much information from those around me simply because it would bore them insufferably — they do not want to know how my geraniums are doing or what my cat had for breakfast. It does not follow that these are my secrets.

The case of privacy has perhaps as much in common with this kind of restraint as with actual secrecy. We divulge information according to whether or not we think the circumstances appropriate. Thus if I find myself in the kind of club or theatre where a compère calls out, "Is there anyone in the audience from Newcastle?", I keep quiet, and this is partly a matter of personal privacy. It falls somewhere between the desire not to bore people with unsolicited accounts of my background (restraint) and the kind of concealment which I might engage in if I were a spy pretending actually to be from Leningrad when interviewed by the K.G.B. (secrecy). As a recent writer on secrecy has said:

> Privacy and secrecy overlap whenever the efforts . . . rely on hiding. But privacy need not hide; and secrecy hides far more than what is private.[2]

Privacy as Anonymity

It has been suggested by some recent writers on data protection that anonymity is the characteristic feature of privacy:

> A "right to privacy" . . . is closely allied with our sense of anonymity. We may commute for years — same train, same compartment, same fellow-travellers — and yet the man to whom we reveal our hopes, our opinions, our beliefs, our business and domestic joys and crises remains "The chap who gets on at Dorking with *The Times* and a pipe; I don't know who he *is*". And he does not know who we *are*, because we have never exchanged names, and thus the necessary communication and release of our private concerns is accomplished without violation of our privacy. In our anonymity lies our security.[3]

It is no doubt true that there is a connection to be made here. One way of maintaining one's privacy is sometimes to remain anonymous. Yet there must be a great deal more to it than this. One does not always, or even usually, regard it as an invasion of privacy when one is asked to give one's name — even by a total stranger. Furthermore, one's privacy is often felt to be under threat in cases where anonymity is preserved. A person's name is probably the one piece of information concerning him or her which is utterly common property, and can be learned, passed on, and commented upon without any suggestion of prying, snooping, or any other form of impropriety. We give our names casually to people at parties, at work, on holiday, in bars and clubs; we give it to receptionists, clerks, waiters, shopkeepers, and even (despite the above) to people on trains. Anonymity, when it is important, is more likely to be a means to the end of upholding one's privacy than to be that in which the privacy actually consists. If a person does not know my name, there is a great deal more that he cannot find out about me until he learns it. He cannot, for example, discover my address or telephone number, or look me up in any file or document. If I am interested in privacy I may have good reason to withhold my name in certain circumstances, just as I may also have good reason to withhold my car registration number or the name of the company for which I work. It does not follow that some-one's possession of any of these bits of information in itself constitutes a violation of my privacy. Anonymity and privacy are conceptually quite distinct, and it will be wise to keep them separate here.

A 'Private Sphere'?

If the concept of anonymity alone is not capable of illuminating that of privacy, it might perhaps be supposed that a slight modification of the approach just indicated will give us what we want. That is, it may be thought that privacy can still be characterized as the mere withholding of certain information, but that it is not as simple as anonymity, and will need to include in the category of the "private" a number of other things, such as those to which I have remarked that one's name can give someone access.

On this view, our lives are divided into a public and a private sphere, and privacy may be defined as the freedom of the latter from violation by others. This is, I think, a popular picture of the nature of privacy among those who have thought sufficiently about the issue to have some sort of theory about it, yet not enough to be aware of the de-ficiency of this view.

When we begin to ask what things would have to be included in this "private sphere" of life, it is difficult to give any clear answers. What has been said above regarding one's name seems to go also for such things as one's address, age, marital status, state of health, and to some extent even one's income and financial circumstances. There seems to be no one fact of this kind which one wishes to remain unknown to everyone. Even if not all candidates for inclusion in the private sphere turn out to be things which we would gossip about to chance acquaintances, it is almost certainly the case that there are people to whom we would be happy to divulge the information without regarding it as a breach of our privacy. There is practically nothing significant about us which is not known, and quite rightly known, by someone or other.

But what if someone were to collect not just the odd bit of information of this kind concerning me, but all the information which might be seen as falling into this category? Here I would like to say two things. First, there are people who possess all of this sort of information about me, and the same is true of most individuals in our society. The important thing is that there are very few such people — wife, parents, close friends — and that I know who they are. If the same cluster of facts were known by someone outside this close circle, I might feel uncomfortable.

And if I had reason to believe that they were all known to someone of whose identity I was not aware, I would feel more uncomfortable still.

Secondly, this does not apply solely to information which falls into any one particular category which can be labeled private; if someone begins systematically to assemble information of any kind about me without some fairly good reason, I will be alarmed in much the same way, and this will be partly a matter of protecting my privacy.

These facts should provide a clue to a more adequate understanding of the concept, and I shall return to them later. What has been established here is that privacy is not to be looked for in some single, sacrosanct area of one's life which can be demarcated from the rest. Often things of great personal importance to us can be known to others in the right circumstances without our privacy being threatened. Conversely even the most trivial pieces of information, picked up by the wrong person or in the wrong spirit, can constitute such a threat. All this does not entail that privacy has nothing to do with the withholding of information, as it very clearly has. All I have argued is that it is not to do with the drawing of a blanket cover over some specific class of facts. To indicate how this approach to privacy is likely to mislead us, I shall consider a more sophisticated and plausible, though still importantly mistaken, analysis.

Privacy as Control

In Britain the Younger Report on privacy (1972) consciously avoided offering any general definition of the concept. However, the more recent Lindop Committee on data protection had the following to say in its report (1978):

> The Younger Committee had to deal with the whole field of privacy. Our task has been to deal with that of data protection. In fact, the two fields overlap, and the area of overlap can be called "information privacy" or, better, "data privacy". It is an important area. . . . But it is not by itself the whole field of data protection, and we have had to consider some matters which do not directly raise questions of privacy. However, we found it useful to examine the concept of data privacy, and its implications and consequences. For this purpose we have used the term data privacy to mean the individual's claim to control the circulation of data about himself.[4]

The overlap referred to here forms the subject matter of this chapter, and I shall follow the committee in adopting the term "data privacy" in talking about it. But I believe the above definition, though moving in the right direction, still misses the mark somewhat. One reason for this is its sweeping breadth. How could we possibly bring about a situation in which every individual is in total control of the transmission of facts about him or her? We do not normally think that our privacy has been violated in every case in which facts about us are circulated without our consent. In very few such cases does one authorize the communication personally, and very often one is completely unaware that it has occurred.

Here I am thinking primarily of the more traditional and small-scale methods of information gathering, storage, and transmission. Friends and relatives pass on news concerning me, my colleagues discuss my work and other related affairs, and many people with whom I deal keep some information concerning me which may be quite harmlessly conveyed to those with a legitimate use for it or purpose in requiring it. There are, then, normal and reasonable ways in which information about persons may be circulated independently of the control of those persons. The fact that this could be achieved on a larger scale and more efficiently by the use of computer technology is only worrying if there is some independent reason for not wishing this to happen.

I suggest that what we are apt to object to is not so much lack of control over data which concerns us, as the possibility of the wrong bits of information getting into the wrong hands, or getting there by the wrong means or through the wrong channels. Typical reactions of this kind are, "What did you have to tell him *that* for?", "What has it got to do with *her*?", "I had rather he hadn't heard it from *them*." The wider significance of these examples will become evident in a later section, in which I offer my own account of data privacy and what constitutes a breach of it. I shall also have more to say later concerning the subject's control over data; I have suggested here that this is not essentially bound up with privacy, but that does not imply that it is not important. Next, however, I shall look briefly at another concept which has been employed in connection with privacy, and which I think will help to lead us in the right direction.

The Notion of Inviolate Personality

In another well-known paper on the concept of privacy in (United States) law, Edward J. Bloustein appeals to the notion of "inviolate personality," about which he says:

> I take the principle of "inviolate personality" to point the individual's independence, dignity and integrity; it defines man's essence as a unique and self-determining being.[5]

The importance of bringing in such ideas as dignity and integrity is that, in contrast to the last two chapters, we are talking now about data protection as an end, and not merely as a means. In defending the liberty of people against totalitarianism, or securing justice for them against the errors of officialdom, data protection is a means: it is an important means, but still only a means. When we turn from liberty and justice to consider the dignity and sense of integrity of the person, the possibility arises of a kind of harm being done to him or her simply in virtue of such surveillance and not by means of it. One writer has expressed the affront to personal dignity brought about by data technology as follows:

> My electronic image in the machine may be more real than I am. It is rounded; it is complete; it is retrievable; it is predictable in statistical terms. . . . I am a mess; and I don't know what to do. The machine knows better — in statistical terms. Thus is my reality less real than my mirror image in the store. That fact diminishes me.[6]

Not all of us would feel exactly like this about the situation, perhaps. However, it illustrates well the point that privacy is not just a matter of how information might be used. As I suggested earlier in this chapter, it is not only when data is actually used against us that we sense a grievance, and it is not essentially a matter of weighing consequences at all. The argument here is not that possible misuse, either malicious or non-malicious, makes the practice of data storage dangerous, but rather that a wrong may in some cases be done to the subject of the information by the practice itself, independently of how the information in question might or might not be used.

What in the situation can be at fault, given that no actual ill consequences need be foreseen, and that information need not even be made public, for such an objection to stand? How does inviolate personality relate to other considerations raised so far, such as the ideas of information getting "into the wrong hands" or going "through the wrong channels"? It is time to say something more positive about the nature of privacy.

Privacy and the Role Structure

A person appears in a variety of different capacities or "social roles," for example, those of child, parent, friend, husband or wife, employer or employee, and so on. Which social role is in question at a given time will depend on whom the occupant of the roles is dealing with, and in what sort of situation.

Before going any farther it will be wise to make clear two things concerning the concept of social role as used here, to avoid misunderstanding and to forestall certain kinds of objection. First, talking about roles in this sense has nothing essentially to do with acting in the theatrical sense, though the word role in sociology and psychology was originally a metaphor borrowed from the stage. To say that someone is playing, acting, or occupying a role in our context is by no means to suggest that he is pretending to be something which he or she is not. In the present sense, in fact, one can only play a certain role successfully if one actually *is* the thing in question. The idea that role-playing is connected with insincerity in some special way is based on a confusion. We are tempted to think that a person plays a role successfully if he is able to convince the "audience" that he or she is what he explicitly or implicitly claims to be (a confidence-trickster posing as an insurance broker, or an out-of-work egotist pretending to be a tycoon). Insofar as the original meaning of "role" involves pretence, it is not pretence of this kind: the actor who plays Richard III does not aim at convincing us that he *is* Richard III. Deceit is neither necessary nor sufficient for a successful performance, and the same holds in the case of the genuine social agent. The actor who plays the part of a priest on the stage succeeds if he is good at representing a priest; the genuine article succeeds if he is good at being a priest.

The second point is that a role does not have to possess any sort of official character. When roles are mentioned, it is tempting to think of such things as "policeman," "member of Parliament," "adjutant," and so on. It is essential, however, to remember that there are many more informal kinds of role which are less well-defined, and may even include oddities such as "unsuccessful applicant," "hopeful suitor," or "innocent bystander." In fact the concept of role in the broad sense employed here includes any social position to which a learned repertoire of behavior tends to be attached, both on the part of the occupant of that position and of others vis-à-vis that person.

It is sometimes plausibly suggested that these roles, if we interpret the notion of role broadly as above, collectively constitute the occupant's identity, at least in one sense of identity. This is the social or sociological sense, rather than the philosopher's strict numerical one. (Notice I am not saying that these roles constitute the person one is, or anything of this sort, but merely that they constitute what it is for a particular person to have the social identity which he or she has.)

Regarding an individual seen as the occupant of a social role, there is information to which only someone standing in the appropriate role-relation can be expected to have access. (By role-relation I mean a relation in which one person stands to another by virtue of the respective roles occupied by the two persons.) There is, for example, information about me which my bank manager possesses but which my employer does not, there is information which both of these possess but which my doctor does not, and much to which my doctor has access but the former do not, and so on. As I have pointed out earlier, however, there is probably little significant information about me which is not possessed by somebody or other.

Yet this last fact does not worry me unduly. What would worry me is the idea that some person (other than someone to whom I stand in a very close and perhaps unique role-relation, such as my wife) had access to *all* this information, or that such information were distributed indiscriminately. A part, then, of what is essential to the integrity of a person's social identity as seen "from the inside" is not some special set of facts to which only he or she has access, nor the exercise of total control over the information relating to him or her, but rather that access to particular information is systematically related in the appropriate way to the network of social relationships in which that person stands to others by virtue of their places in the role structure. *A breach of privacy can be said to have occurred wherever the flow of information becomes divorced from the social role structure in some way.* For want of a better label we might call this the Short Circuit Effect.

To accept a social role is to accept that certain relationships will hold between myself and the occupants of other roles. It is to assent to the appropriateness of a particular pattern of interaction. Once I have accepted a role I can have no legitimate grievance as long as my relations (in that role) with others follow the understood pattern which attaches to it. If this pattern is departed from, however, I may indeed have a grievance. If I do business with an insurance company, I can hardly object to their knowing the value of my possessions. Nor can I complain when my confessor asks me about my sins, or my doctor asks me to take my clothes off. But my privacy certainly will be threatened if my doctor begins investigating how much I am worth, if the insurance man becomes interested in my sins, or if a priest asks me to take off my clothes.

Not all social roles, of course, are explicitly chosen or even chosen at all, but this fact makes no essential difference. There is a difference between choosing a role and accepting a role. I accept the role of son which defines a particular relationship vis-à-vis my parents, though I did not choose it in the first place. Conversely a man who leaves his wife is refusing to accept a role, though it was he who chose it.

But what of a person who does not accept the role in question? An anarchist, for example, might go so far as to reject the title citizen in a society such as ours; he will certainly reject the role of subject. As a result he may consider that, among other things, he is not obliged to fill in a census form, and that to make him do so would violate his privacy. This question goes far beyond the scope of this book, for it involves far more than merely privacy. It will suffice to sketch an answer for present purposes. There are some roles which it is open to us to accept or reject, and some which (on most views) it is not. Where we draw the line will vary from one society to another, and over time. In some cultures it is considered morally permissible for children to abandon or disown their parents; in others it is not. Similarly some people maintain that it is morally obligatory to accept and fulfil the role of elector (that is, to vote in elections when entitled, and not to do so frivolously), while others deny this. What will always hold, however, is that where we think there is a moral duty to accept a particular role, we will not recognize as legitimate a grievance which arises out of a claim to reject it. On the other hand, where we regard acceptance or rejection as a matter for individual choice, we will recognize such a grievance as legitimate. (A mother who abandons a new-born baby cannot sensibly be thought innocent on the grounds that she rejects the role of mother, but a person can reasonably refuse to pay for unsolicited goods on the grounds that he rejects the role of customer which some high-pressure salesman is trying to foist on him.)

Returning to the question of data privacy, we can now see why Bloustein's notion of "inviolate personality" is a move in the right direction. Remember, I have not said that our social roles are what constitute our personality, but there is a very strong connection. I have distinguished between (a) personal identity, in the traditional philosophical sense, (b) personality, which is both an informal and a psychological notion, and (c) identity, in the social and sociological senses. The philosophical concept of personal identity is not in question here, but an attack on the integrity of one's social identity is one kind of threat to one's personality when these are, as I have put it, seen from the inside.

One final word before concluding this section. I have appeared to assume up to now, as is assumed by most writers on this topic, that privacy is somehow essentially tied up with individualism. Constant reference is made to the individual and the person as the subject of privacy. Yet this need not be the case. There is a perfectly good sense in which a family, for example, might require privacy *qua* family. Even an entire culture may, under certain circumstances, be said to enjoy privacy in a global context, and this privacy could be threatened by changes in the relationships between that culture or society and the rest of the world. Here the situation is essentially the same, though superficially very different. A family or an entire society can hardly be said to occupy a social role in the way in which individuals do within a society. Yet it is still true that there are accepted relationships which hold between societies (mutual cooperation, alliances, trade relations, cargo cults), and that an entire culture can be harmed by outsiders riding roughshod over such understood patterns. Single-minded information-seekers can do much the same kind of damage to the privacy of a society in these circumstances as a different sort of technological snooper can do to that of an individual in more familiar ones. Collective data privacy will not play a large part in the remainder of the discussion, which is to be pursued in the next chapter, but it is well to bear these points in mind throughout.

6. More about Privacy

In the last chapter I outlined a theory about the nature of privacy, particularly as it relates to the handling of information on people. I suggested also that privacy is among what we may regard as the natural human rights, in that it is a quasi-biological need which we experience as human beings. Thus any choice which we make regarding our collective future will, unless human nature suddenly somehow changes overnight, have to embody the idea of privacy among its values, and to incorporate norms aimed at guaranteeing its observance.

In this chapter I would like to look at some concrete proposals regarding what kind of principles might be appropriate; to see how such principles apply to the situation as we find it today; and finally to relate all this to the theoretical concerns of the preceding chapter and the final chapter.

Putting Theory into Practice

A case of invasion of privacy with regard to personal information would, on the account I offered in the last chapter, be one in which information became available to people or through channels which could reasonably be regarded as inappropriate in the circumstances. I referred to this previously as the Short Circuit Effect, and I shall use that term here too.

So far, however, I have said very little about what is to count as "inappropriate in the circumstances," beyond appealing to the idea of an accepted role structure and of understood role relations. Clearly this rather theoretical notion will not suffice to do the job on its own and needs fleshing out with some content. Nor will my somewhat cartoon-like examples of doctors, priests, and bank managers be adequate.

A certain amount of vagueness is, however, quite in order here, for the norms regarding what is and is not appropriate vary from one society to another and from one time to another, and are bound to remain to some extent a matter of opinion and speculation, rather than of ascertainable fact. It would be a mistake, therefore, to look for hard and fast rules, and for the most part we must be content with a schematic outline of what a solution would look like. Nevertheless, there are certain principles which need to be incorporated in one form or another into any system of social practices that gives a place to the concept of data privacy. None of these principles is original, and indeed it would tend to go against much that I have already said if they were. I propose:

(1) The recipient of personal information must have a legitimate use for it.

The significance of this is twofold. On the one hand, it affirms the necessity of maintaining a link between possession/access and use, which is far from trivial. Information ought not to be gathered and retained "just in case" a use should arise for it. We need not insist that every scrap of data obtained should have a determinate purpose which is minutely specifiable. This would be absurd. All that is involved is a general requirement that there be a connection of an intelligible kind: my employer needs my home address not for any specific purpose, nor out of misplaced curiosity or any other dubious motive, but simply because it is the kind of thing he is likely to have a legitimate use for. This brings me, on the other hand, to the second point about (1). I have made use of the word legitimate in the condition, which may seem to beg the question. By legitimate I do not merely mean "lawful," for part of what we are trying to determine is what the law on these matters ought to be. I use it here to mean something more like "honest," though even this does not go quite far enough. I shall therefore suggest a second principle in order to provide some further substance to the requirement:

(2) The purposes of the recipient in acquiring the information must be connected in a positive way with the interests of the subject of that information.

One difficulty with this principle is its apparent elasticity. It would be quite possible for a company compiling lists of potential clients to claim that it is in the interests of the individuals concerned to have the company's product or service brought to their attention. A simple way of interpreting the criterion, therefore, would be to appeal to the hypothetical wishes of the subject. If we ask, in a given case, whether the person in question would or would not say, if queried, that he wanted another double-glazing catalogue delivered to his house, we will know whether or not the above requirement is fulfilled.

Furthermore, the notion of being "connected in a positive way with the interests of the subject" is intended to be very inclusive. It is not actually in my interest that gas-meter readers come into my house and work out what I owe the gas company; but it is in my interest that there be a gas company and that I subscribe to that set of arrangements of which meter-reading is an integral part. The same will be true of many of my relations with the state.

It may, however, still be objected that by no means all the information about a person transmitted from one agency to another can be expected to conform to this condition, however broadly understood. What about information passed on to law-enforcement agencies for the purpose of bringing about the capture of dangerous criminals? (A famous instance was the apprehension of the murderer Dr. Crippen as he attempted to flee from Britain to Canada in 1910, as a result of a radio message from a ship in the Atlantic — was his privacy thus violated, and must we therefore condemn what was done?). I would like to say two things about this. The first is that I have nowhere suggested that the right to privacy is an absolute right. I believe, in fact, that it is quite clearly a *prima facie* right, which may be overridden in certain circumstances. This is not meant as a gesture toward consequentialism, and I am not claiming that rights are to be overridden whenever it is judged beneficial to do so. A *prima facie* right is a conditional one, and if the relevant conditions do not hold, neither does the right. To see that this is the case, we have only to consider any activity A, and to ask whether one has a "right to do A"; then to ask further whether one has the "right to the privacy to do A." Given that the answer to the former question will sometimes be no, the answer to the latter cannot always be yes, otherwise anyone could claim the right to do anything he liked, simply by ensuring that any means by which he could be prevented from doing it would constitute a breach of his privacy. We need not worry, then, that some quite (in the circumstances) unexceptionable ways of obtaining information will in fact count as violations of privacy on the account given here — for violations of privacy will sometimes be in order. This is a much more natural solution to the above problem than the alternative, which would be to devise a definition of privacy such that no breach of a person's privacy could ever be justified.

The second thing which I want to say regarding the above objection is that there are cases in which the right of privacy is commonly thought to override even the necessity of efficient law enforcement. In recent debates concerning proposals to extend the police's powers of search, many professional people such as doctors and lawyers have expressed disquiet regarding the possibility that they might be obliged to open their files to police investigation. The confidentiality of the confessional, and its immunity even from such inquiries, is notorious. The justification here, however, is that the existence of relationships of trust depends on confidentiality, and to abuse this would effectively destroy the very possibility of them: once priests start turning murderers over to the police, no one will ever confess a murder again. Just how far this somewhat Kantian point will take us, and whether it is sufficient on its own to justify such absolute injunctions, need not be settled here. What does arise out of the foregoing, however, is the possibility of formulating a third principle of data privacy along the following lines: .

(3) The availability of personal information must be inversely related to the degree of confidentiality under which it was originally obtained.

The fourth principle which I would like to suggest is very straightforward and relates to things which have been said in earlier chapters regarding subject access to data:

(4) The subject must have some practicable means of discovering what information about him or her has been transmitted to whom, and must have access to it.

This fourth condition does little more than expand on the gloss which we gave to requirement (2), where it was suggested that the hypothetical consent of the subject must be capable of being reasonably supposed. Condition (4) will guarantee this, as well as ensuring that the rationale of (3) will hold, for confidentiality must not only be maintained but be seen to be maintained if relationships of trust are to exist.

The principles outlined in this section are a minimum set of conditions for the existence of some form of data privacy. They are presented as individually necessary conditions, though they are not individually sufficient and probably not jointly sufficient either. To put this in terms of the violation of data privacy, the failure of any one of these conditions to apply will be individually sufficient for what I have called a short-circuit of information (though such an occurrence may often be quite trivial), while the failure of any given condition will not be necessary for this, and neither, probably, will their joint failure.

This list of principles places the onus of proof on the person who wishes to transfer personal data from one information store or agency to another. In other words, the principles are weighted in favor of a presupposition that *personal information gathered and stored for one purpose must not, without some strong overriding reason, be used for another.* What kind of thing is to be regarded as a strong, overriding reason is open to debate at this stage. Clearly it must be a specific reason applying in a particular case, and not a blanket provision, or it will contravene the underlying presumption. For example, if the release of a confidential medical record on a person is requested by detectives investigating a crime, some explanation would need to be given which represented the circumstances as exceptional — some explanation, that is, other than simply that a crime was being investigated. The fact that we are not as yet certain what would constitute exceptional circumstances (strength of the suspicion, seriousness of the crime, unavailability of the subject to give his consent?) does not alter the presumption on which the above principles rest. This is simply to register the fact that we will require good reasons for allowing the use of personal data collected for one purpose to be made available for another, rather than requiring good reasons for preventing it. This presupposition follows, I suggest, from what I said at the outset of this chapter concerning the reasonableness of counting privacy among basic human rights. Rights, as I have observed, need not always be absolute and inviolable, but they do serve to mark the direction in which our prejudices (in the best sense) ought to run, and to establish on which side the burden of proof will lie.

We will return to the above principles and their consequences in a later chapter. For the moment let us turn from these somewhat abstract considerations to see how what I have said so far in this chapter relates to the current situation, and what practical relevance it has for us now and in the future.

The Position Today

If I am correct in analyzing the idea of data privacy in terms of what I have called the Short Circuit Effect, it is not difficult to see what follows. As we have seen in chapter 1, the increasing incidence of this effect is one of the most striking and pervasive concomitants of the technological revolution. It is not only the quantity of information acquired and stored which is thought to be alarming about today's situation; it is not only its possible indiscriminateness, inaccuracy, or openness to abuse. It is also the ease with which, in sophisticated systems, data can be diverted from channels which occupy some recognized and legitimate place in the social network, into those which do not and which may rightly be viewed with some suspicion. This is one of the points where we can see a very direct connection with the considerations raised in the first chapter regarding the way in which technical features of the computerized systems themselves give rise to ethical problems by changing the social pattern of data flow.

Many of the sources of concern which were referred to in the early part of the book will now be seen as falling into the present category and as turning on the issue of privacy. A few examples may establish that the phenomenon we are discussing is not a mere invention or chimera.

When the possibility of setting up a central data bank was under discussion in the United States, a number of disturbing facts came to light. Some of them were summarized as follows:

> Records about an individual are passed too freely among agencies. In many places a bank report or a detailed high school record, including medical reports, is easily made available to a prospective employer. When an individual consents to the release of records about him this should remove liability. But there are many situations when he does not know that the information about him is being circulated, or he cannot object to the release.[1]

To render the subject manageable we may begin by thinking of ways of dividing up the relevant cases.

First, there is an important distinction between short circuits of information which occur by legal and above-board means and those which are brought about by "back door" methods (methods which do not involve the consent of the original holder of the data, or are irregular in some other way). As I stressed earlier, we are not concerned so much with data *security* as with data *protection*. For this reason I shall have little to say about illegitimate data transactions, and will concentrate on those transactions which are at least candidates for being considered above-board, whatever the actual legal situation in any given country at the time of writing.

A second distinction turns on the nature of the source which divulges the information, and the identity of the person or agency to which it is transferred. One or both of them may, for example, be a government agency. The British government alone administers, in one form or other, well over 200 separate computerized databases, apparently with the very minimum of control over what information may be switched between them. This includes information collected by the Inland Revenue, security forces, Customs and Excise, the Census, the Department of Health and Social Security, the Department of Employment, vehicle and television licensing authorities, and the National Health Service. An example of the indiscriminate swapping of data between such agencies is the alleged handing-over, in large numbers, of confidential health records on abortion patients, in order that the police may identify those which contravene the Abortion Act and prosecute offenders. Dr. John Dawson, the head of the professional division of the British Medical Association, commented, "I do not think patients have any idea of how much information about them is already spread through a wide network."

On the other hand, one or both of the organizations in question may be a private commercial enterprise. The system of credit-rating agencies mentioned earlier, for instance, operates entirely between private concerns. Into the same category fall those agencies that exist to provide lists of names and addresses which may be used for the purpose of unsolicited mailing. There are about 20 such agencies in Britain, selling details of potential customers in a variety of categories corresponding to the services offered by clients:

> One catalogue, for example, offers details of 5,000 executive secretaries. "Because of their executive and influential roles, they have a considerable influence on the activities and buying habits of their bosses," says the catalogue.
> Or there are 10,000 businessmen . . . men, in all walks of life, from the 50+ age group, whose names and home addresses can be supplied.
> What other categories can be got at? Well . . . 30,000 winter sports enthusiasts, who purchase ski equipment with an average value of £50 and £100; 1,000 Senior Service officers, 52,000 theatre lovers, 150,000 shareholders in public companies, 45,000 directors of newly-formed companies. Even 10,000 affluent Britons abroad.
> All are for rent, and the cost ranges from £35 to £75 per 1,000 names and addresses . . . .[2]

Credit card companies claim that they do not release information on their cardholders for other uses, though such claims are not always believed. It is not just between government agencies, or only between private companies, that such information can be transferred. Sometimes data from government records will find its way onto those of private organizations, and quite possibly vice-versa. Data from police computers has been known to be divulged to a subject's prospective employer or other interested party. Ex-policemen turned private detectives are able, through contacts formed in the police force, to obtain information from police records which may be used in the interests of clients.

A third sort of case concerns bodies which are neither precisely government agencies nor private businesses. Examples are nationalized industries, trade unions, and other semi-voluntary organizations. Clearly once the kinds of agencies in question are identified, the possible permutations of data transactions will be obvious, and it will be needless to dwell on them all. A final example involving all three types of organization is provided by this newspaper extract from early in 1983:

> *"DON'T SELL OUR NAMES" SAYS NUS*
> The National Union of Students is objecting strongly to British Rail's plan to sell names and addresses of student railcard holders to commercial interests. BR has already been criticised by consumer watchdogs for its plans to sell details of senior citizens' railcard holders to an insurance company.[3]

The special problem in many of these cases is that of identifying the point at which an infringement of privacy actually takes place, and who is responsible for it. Take, for instance, the compilation of lists of names, addresses, and so forth for commercial purposes. If we accept that violations of privacy *can* come about in this way, the problem is the following. Much of the information involved in typical cases of this sort is, quite rightly, publicly available. It may be gleaned from documents such as telephone directories, trade handbooks, newspapers, *Who's Who*, and other perfectly respectable sources. There can be nothing illegitimate in looking up the odd entry in these publications. But if this is so, how can there be anything wrong in doing it repeatedly? And if one has a right to all this information, is one not also entitled to piece it together, store it, and "process" it in any way one chooses? Should one wish to sell the data thus collected to others, what can be amiss here, since the others could, had they wished, have come by the information in just the same way themselves? Note that this is not a problem created specifically by computer technology; the same puzzle exists, for example, in the case of saying what constitutes spying, given that much of what is done by spies in foreign countries is simply the putting-together of information which, in its individual parts, is more or less public.

One reason for the puzzlement here is the tacit assumption that if a wrong is done, it must be done by some determinate person, or by a number of persons perpetrating specific contributory wrongs. This will receive a more detailed treatment in a later chapter, when we shall ask what, if anything, is to be done about the state of affairs described. The present chapter merely offers a diagnosis.

For the present, I must turn to a further question which is raised by the foregoing — that of the connection between the facts as described here and the technology which has made such a situation possible.

The Connection with Neutrality

I argued in chapter 2 for a distinction between those sorts of technology which are *application-neutral* and those which are not, and also for a further distinction between those which are *policy-neutral* and those which are not. Returning to these categories, I shall try to answer the question of just what role is played by the enabling technology in the threat to privacy described in this chapter.

I have argued for the view of computer technology as being relatively neutral in the senses outlined in chapter 2 — as neutral as anything can be, given the inherent limitations on such neutrality. Yet even if information technology does not come complete with a set of applications or policies, it is a mistake to think that all the consequences of our actions are a matter of policy. Many of them are neither intended nor foreseen.

Given that the system which threatens the individual's privacy is made possible by present-day computer technology, has this technology played an active or a passive role in the process? Has it played a part in shaping policy, other than making policies easier to carry out? Remember the kind of examples we considered in order to make this distinction in chapter 2. To own a gun is to possess a piece of technology which has certain more-or-less specifiable applications (it can only be actually used for shooting at things), but which is policy-neutral inasmuch as owning a gun need not make it especially likely that I will commit myself to any particular courses of action, even a hypothetical one. I may use it for shooting intruders, or I may just wish to rely on threatening them with it, or I might merely want it to be known that I keep a gun so as to make intrusions less probable, or again I may simply use it for firing at pigeons or tin cans. By contrast, certain kinds of missile now in existence are not policy-neutral in this way. A missile whose only function is to destroy enemy missiles still on the ground is a piece of technology which comes with a built-in policy — that of the first strike — for this is its only use, and to commit oneself to the device is *ipso facto* to embrace the policy.

With regard to the violation of privacy I again wish to insist on the fundamental neutrality of information technology, in the sense that it does not of itself force a particular range of policies, or even specific types of application. Its potentialities are pretty much open-ended. In this respect the whole apparatus (at least in its hardware aspect) of link-ups, terminals, databases, data banks, on-line information, and telecommunications which was discussed in chapter 1 is merely a set of passive instruments in our hands.

To say this, however, is not to say that one policy is therefore as likely to be pursued as another. It may be that certain courses of action made possible by a given technological development are ones in favor of which, or against which, people will have a natural prejudice or inclination. (High-speed travel is entirely neutral as between the choice of holidaying in the south of France or in Siberia — it makes them both equally easy — but we know in practice which alternative people will generally choose.) Moreover, to say that technology of this sort is policy-neutral is not necessarily to say that it is neutral as between a number of mutually exclusive options. It may be the case that the possibilities thus opened up are such that they may all be pursued without undue inconvenience. Technology, we have said, cannot be held responsible for what it merely makes *possible*, but for what in practice it makes *inevitable*, and it will never be inevitable that we follow up every possible use for our inventions.

No positive pressure toward privacy-violating policies and techniques actually arises out of the available hardware. The pressure, if any, exists in the decision-makers themselves, in the form of idle curiosity, or of a thirst for the kind of knowledge which creates power, comprehensiveness, or merely access to some private information which others do not possess, that exists to some extent in all of us. It is what has been referred to as the "If we *can* do it then we *must*" mentality, and comes into the category (along with simple error, which was discussed in chapter 4) of *the human factor*.

The human factor is not the only influence at work inclining a fairly neutral kind of technology to be applied in connection with a given range of applications and policies. I have talked also about the cultural factor — the part played by the social, political, and economic background against which these decisions have to be taken. This, as we have seen, takes us another step from being able to talk about moral neutrality in connection with technology of almost any kind. The consequences of this, when the technology is information technology and the moral issue is privacy, should be fairly obvious. Clearly a culture that already regards it acceptable for citizens to be spied upon and to have particulars of their lives recorded either by public or by private agencies will be more inclined to seize upon the new technology for this purpose than one which does not already have these features. In the former case those who find this sort of surveillance undesirable will have a much harder time resisting it. In short, as we saw in chapter 3 when talking about political oppression in general, something must already have gone wrong in order for our worst fears about information technology to be justified. It is not part of the essential nature of the technology in question that it should be used for these purposes rather than some others. The purposes are "in the eye of the beholder," and how the technology is viewed will depend on the cultural spectacles through which one views it. From the point of view of the cultural factor, therefore, the safeguards needed to ensure that information technology is not used to invade personal privacy are those which are required to ensure a society in which human rights are respected in general. These go much wider than merely privacy acts and data-protection legislation. More will be said about this in chapter 10.

Consequentialism and Privacy

I turn now to a brief consideration of how the concept of privacy stands with regard to the wider background of ethical theory. One thing which has emerged in this chapter is that objections to uses of data technology which turn on the privacy issue do not always relate simply to the consequences of what is done. It is not only the possible uses of stored information, nor even its disclosure, which is seen as potentially violating the rights of subjects to privacy, but its very existence. That is, it is the practices themselves and not merely their effects which may sometimes trespass on the privacy of individuals.

The word consequentialism is often used to describe certain systems of ethics. Roughly speaking, an ethical theory is said to be consequentialist if it judges an action to be good or bad, right or wrong, solely by virtue of its consequences. Utilitarianism is the best-known moral system which falls into this category, holding that the supreme ethical principle is that of maximizing "utility," normally understood as human happiness, though it is also defined by some writers as pleasure or fulfilment or satisfaction, as some other concept designed to cover everything regarded as ultimately desirable. Its classic formulation is embodied in J.S. Mill's principle that "actions are right in proportion as they tend to promote happiness, wrong as they tend to produce the reverse of happiness."[4]

Consequentialist theories have been subjected to a large number of well-worn objections. The point I wish to make is that the issue of privacy, for the above reasons, provides a very striking instance of the kind of counterexample to which consequentialism is prone. In contrast to the problems which we looked at in chapters 3 and 4, we are not dealing just with a question of identifying certain consequences which may ensue when information about people is circulated in certain ways, and of preventing such consequences. These matters are, as we have seen, thorny enough; but in dealing with privacy a new level of complexity is introduced. If it were possible to give an analysis, *what* consequences might be supposed to be in question? What commodity is it which is intended to be maximized, or its absence minimized, in the maintenance of privacy? The initial and apparently obvious response may be to say that the situation is no different from how it would be (from a consequentialist point of view) in any other case of harm done to persons. The good to be maximized is the individual's happiness, and it is the unhappiness caused by the privacy-invading activities of others which the good consequentialist will seek to reduce.

But consider. If the harm done is meant to be cashed out as distress caused to the subjects of the information transmitted, what of the many cases in which the subject is unaware that the information even exists? Has any harm been done or not? If it has, it cannot lie in any effect on the mental state of the subject, in its making him or her unhappy, nervous, anxious, or the like. But if it has not, there can be harmless invasions of people's privacy — indeed only *known* violations (i.e., known to the subject) could be considered objectionable at all. But if the latter is the case, why should anyone worry about undisclosed data transactions? And are these not precisely the ones about which we are most concerned? On such a consequentialist account surely we ought to cooperate in ensuring that they remain undiscovered? Either way, the consequentialist will not have explained the objection to violations of privacy in terms of effects on the well-being of subjects.

The consequentialist may, however, resort to a familiar move in arguments of this sort, which is to claim that the harm done by the undisclosed instances lies in the cumulative, long-term anxiety caused to everyone by the knowledge that undisclosed invasions of privacy may be occurring. Reducing the likelihood of these occurrences will reduce the anxiety.

One response to this argument might be to point out that the consequentialist would at least be forced to accept that if all instances could be kept secret, then no harm would have been done. This point, though it carries a certain weight, will not impress everyone. Sophisticated utilitarians such as R.M. Hare are apt to reply that the contingency is so remote as to paralyze our moral intuition altogether; in other words, an ordinary, sensible person will simply not know what to make of such an outlandish situation — perhaps if the secrecy were *total*, then it *would* be all right.[5] None of the characteristic effects of assaults on our privacy — embarrassment, resentment, feeling of claustrophobia — would ever result from such a state of affairs. What would be the problem? Maybe it is only the probability of violations becoming public knowledge which creates the harm.

Unfortunately this defense, although it can perhaps deal with some farfetched counterexamples, does not answer the most central charges against the above refinement of consequentialism. First, this refinement has the effect of shifting the locus of harm from where it actually lies to where the consequentialist perhaps thinks it ought to be. An analogy will make this point clearer. Suppose that I were deceiving my best friend by sleeping with his wife un-beknown to him. Given that this activity is not blameless, where does the harm lie, and to whom is it done? If it is a wrong done to *him*, it cannot consist in the effect on his happiness or peace of mind, for it has no such effect. It must, for the consequentialist, be wrong only in virtue of the anxiety caused to husbands in general through knowing of the widespread practice of marital infidelity and betrayal of friendship. (In which case, it will only be wrong because it is harmful if indulged in by a sufficient number of people, like walking across the grass.) But we all know that the harm done cannot be described simply like this. It is my friend, in his state of blissful ignorance, whom I have wronged and not society as a whole, at least primarily. Nor is it a tiny contribution to a vast and nebulous harm — it is an individual and specific wrong. To deny this is to fly in the face of our moral experience; but it is this which the consequentialist is in such cases led to deny. Consequentialism cannot cope with states of blissful ignorance, and the same is equally true when the ignorance is ignorance of attacks on our privacy.

Secondly, it remains to be explained why even the public knowledge that undisclosed invasions of privacy occur should produce any anxiety if we cannot attribute any harm to these undisclosed incidents independently. Why should there be any harm in contemplating that which itself causes no harm? Here the consequentialist wants to put the cart before the horse. His account in terms of indirect harm caused by public knowledge of the practices in question must ultimately rise on the back of some account of direct harm involved in the practices themselves.

A last resort of the consequentialist is, of course, to accept that the invasion of someone's privacy does constitute a wrong in itself, and to declare that privacy is simply of those things which, in the consequentialist calculus, is to be optimized. At this point the distinction between consequentialist and non-consequentialist accounts begins to break down. To say that spreading personal information about someone indiscriminately is wrong because of its consequences, and then to describe those consequences as a violation of privacy, is no more illuminating than to say that murder is wrong in virtue of its consequences, and then to say that by the latter we mean no more than the death of an innocent person at the hands of another (or whatever). In both cases the former *constitutes* the latter rather than causing it.

I have dwelt on the connection between privacy and consequentialism for two reasons. On the one hand, it throws light on the special interest of the concept of privacy for the moral philosopher. On the other, it underlines the great diversity of the problems which are raised by the ethics of information technology, and their resistance to being treated according to any stock theory. The diversity is a feature of ethics in general. Those who would have us believe that anything which can go wrong in the whole range of our moral experience must be wrong for the same reason, will always come up with a rationale which is either vacuous or unconvincing. More specifically we must beware of glib arguments in the field of information ethics, which by their concentration on one preferred facet of a situation blind us to less obvious but perhaps more sensitive areas of concern, such as privacy, which are no less genuine and worthy of attention.

7. The Non-Human Face of Technology

A popular complaint regarding computers and information technology is that they somehow result in an environment which is alien, unfriendly, or inhuman. Such ideas are often very vague, and even those who hold them would often be at a loss to sharpen them up. Nevertheless, they must be taken seriously: partly because they do genuinely affect the ways in which people react to the new technology and partly because one can intuitively grasp and sympathize with the sentiments which such claims express. In order to judge the appropriateness of these attitudes, we must get them into more focus. When we do so, however, we quickly discover no single kind of worry, but several related and overlapping sources of discontent. We will start with the most obvious of them.

Face to Face with the Computer

The most straightforward source of alarm, to some people at least, is the allegedly increasing extent to which the ordinary person has to deal in everyday life not with other human beings, but with computers. This, it is claimed, tends to create an environment which is socially impoverished, bleak, mechanical, impersonal, "non-human" or even "inhuman." The picture painted is of a world where the people with whom we ultimately interact are all faceless, since they hide constantly behind the machines. Up to a point this is true. We do tend more and more to rely on automatic devices for the more trivial of our daily interactions: withdrawing money from the bank, getting tickets to park our cars, paying for petrol, and so on. Yet even the extent to which this is the case is often exaggerated. We do not yet have computerized shopkeepers, policemen, or bar staff. Some of the functions of the first two have, indeed, been taken over by the computer to a certain extent. In the case of barkeepers, market forces would surely soon bring it about that such an idea were unprofitable! Yet in a sense these responses are irrelevant. The issue is not the extent to which the computerization of everyday life has already happened, but whether or not there is a general trend in that

95

direction. Looked at as objectively as possible, it is very hard to deny that there certainly is such a trend.

If there is, what is supposed to be wrong with it? The point of asking this is that it is not clear why the effect of more sophisticated technology should, in itself, be dehumanizing. Think, for example, of all the artists' impressions or comic strip representations of life twenty, fifty, or a hundred, years in the future; not the Orwellian anti-utopias, but the more straightforwardly utopian dreams of the technological planners and of those who share their convictions. The tendency of nearly all such futurology is to present the high-tech as a collection of labor-saving devices that create more leisure and provide the opportunity to spend more time on the traditional and distinctively human activities of life. (The family sits around the pool while the robots handle all the tiresome tasks.) Why do we not feel that this is how things are actually working out?

To the extent that we do not feel this, the reason seems to be connected with the change in our own expectations which the techno-logical boom has itself created. We discover that we can do things faster: money moves around the world at lightning speed, purchases can be made instantly by using telephone and television, library and archive searches which once took weeks may now take seconds, and so on. But instead of drawing the conclusion that we can now do all the things we need to do in less time than before, we tend rather to draw the conclusion that we can now do *more things*. In *Parkinson's Law: Or the Pursuit of Progress*, C. Northcote Parkinson laid down, with characteristic wit, the following principle:

> Work expands so as to fill the time available for its completion. General recognition of this fact is shown in the proverbial phrase, "It is the busiest man who has time to spare." Thus, an elderly lady of leisure can spend the entire day in writing and dispatching a postcard to her niece at Bognor Regis. An hour will be spent in finding the postcard, another in hunting for spectacles, half an hour in a search for the address, an hour and a quarter in composition, and twenty minutes in deciding whether or not to take an umbrella when going to the pillar box in the next street. The total effort that would occupy a busy man for three minutes all told may in this fashion leave another person prostrate after a day of doubt, anxiety, and toil.
> Granted that work (and especially paperwork) is thus elastic in its demands on time, it is manifest that there need be little or no relationship between the work to be done and the size of the staff to

which it may be assigned. A lack of real activity does not, of necessity, result in leisure. A lack of occupation is not necessarily revealed by a manifest idleness.[1]

That this principle holds to a very large extent is beyond question. However, it is not just that the same tasks can be made to take longer. It is also that we can always find more tasks, and can persuade ourselves and each other that they are necessary. Our standards of how long a given task should take and of how necessary it is rise with the ease with which such a task can be performed, and with the time which has been made available for it. Thus there is a danger that the mechanical operations which were once seen as merely more efficient means to certain desirable ends will turn out to generate not more of the ends we desire, but just more and more means. In other words, we may save ourselves time only to do more time-saving things!

Nor is all this wholly unreasonable. On the contrary, it is often dictated by underlying economic forces. Those people who say to themselves, "Good, now that we have these labor-saving gadgets I (or my workforce) can relax and only work one day a week" are hardly likely to compete successfully with those who say, "Good, now I (or may workforce) can do six times as much work each week." So often the pace of life in general is dictated by the pace of economic life — of making a living.

If this is correct the new technology will make not more time and opportunity for the traditional human-oriented activities, but more time for more keyboard-punching, code deciphering, light-pen bleeping, and poking of magnetized cards into slots. If this is not what we want, we had better do something about it. But what? It is not exactly the fault of the technology itself or even of those who design and make it. Clearly what is at work here is once again the human factor in technology: familiar and understandable human tendencies which, when combined with the possibilities created by new technology, bring about strong pressures in a particular direction. This need not be the direction we actually want to go. In this case we are talking about tendencies such as, for example, the wish to conduct our business as efficiently as possible, the urge to spend a significant amount of our time in profitable work (a very real instinct — the frustration of the unemployed is by no means merely financial); the desire to be at least as competitive as the next person, and so forth. In order to make any difference to such a pattern it would be necessary to change a great deal else in our society and in the way we have been led by the intellectual fashions of our era to think about our lives and expectations. I wish to turn now to an aspect of the above that concerns the way people sometimes feel their lives are being made less human, or less than human, by the rise of information technology and its consequences.

All Computerese to Me

We have probably all had the experience of receiving a document something like the fictitious one reproduced in chapter 1. A document, that is, which has been geared to the strict requirements of an information-processing system but which is very little in tune with the requirements and circumstances of the human beings for whose benefit the system is supposed to exist. This aspect of data processing is not confined to the acquisition of information by the system. It crops up also in the way that information comes from such systems and is transmitted to us as the users. A new language seems to have arisen, "computerese," which has nothing to do with any programming language (i.e., with any sort of code which the computer itself would understand). It comes from machines and is intended solely for human consumption, though nothing could be less appropriate for the purpose. Nor is it even made more intelligible when the recipient possesses a measure of computer literacy. To give a personal example, although qualified in computing science I have myself recently received:

a statement from a gas company from which it cannot be ascertained whether I am six pounds in credit with them or owe them six pounds,

an enquiry about a missing library book which quotes only the catalogue number but no title or author, thus making it impossible to hunt for it effectively, and

a bank statement with no way of telling which of the many figures represents the current balance of the account.

Such examples will have a familiar ring to most people. Although we may be tempted to assume unthinkingly that these things are just the necessary price we have to pay for fast and efficient technology, a little reflection will convince us that this is not so. Take a typical example of computerese, and by no means one of the worst. A library sends a request for a book which it calls "JOHNSON B. BETTER CHESS: THE

ELEMENT." The computer has truncated the string of characters forming the title of the book at 35 characters (including spaces). The last three
words of the title should have been THE ELEMENTARY ENDGAME.
Such a truncation will probably not matter much until one finds that one
also has a book by the same Johnson called *Better Chess: The Elementary
Openings*. At this point it begins to seem as though the problem-solving
gadgetry has *given* us a problem. The passive and uninquisitive recipient
will likely assume that the poor computing system can handle nothing
with more than that number of characters. But this is false. Unless it is
unbelievably antiquated, it should have no difficulty with strings of
25,000 characters or more. It is the person responsible for writing the
software who has decided, for reasons of his or her own, to make 35 the
maximum. Similarly it is just about as easy to tell the computer, "WRITE
'Balance brought forward on January 1st'" as it is to tell it, "WRITE
'BBFd 1/1'," which bears more resemblance to what one usually gets.

The idea that anything which comes out of a machine must be
expected to involve a degree of unintelligibility is simply a confusion. A
machine will say exactly what it is told to say — nothing more or less.
Why, then, do we find this kind of computerese increasingly invading
our lives and making things difficult for us, when things ought to be
getting simpler? Surely the computer should be made to serve our ends,
and not vice versa. Yet it seems increasingly that we are being required
to make adjustments and allowances which, if they are convenient at all,
seem to be convenient only from the point of view of the artifact we have
created.

What we are seeing is another aspect of the Human Factor which was
introduced in chapter 2: the aspect which chapter 4 discussed under the
heading of "Passing the Buck." Nothing is convenient or inconve-
nient for a machine (though of course the things which it finds most
difficult to do, i.e., take most time and resources, might be in-
convenient from our point of view). It is the programmer and user of a
machine who experience inconvenience and who are apt to organize the
system in a way which minimizes this inconvenience. However, in
minimizing the inconvenience to themselves they often increase that on
the part of the ultimate user — the client or customer. This pattern is not
altogether unheard of even where computers are not concerned. The
difference is that the technology provides the lazy programmer or
operator the best possible defense against uninformed criticism. Since
the vast majority of people are still uninformed about information

technology and likely to remain so for the foreseeable future, owing to the expanding amount that there is to know about it, this defense tends to be pretty secure.

About the human instinct to save time and work wherever possible there is not a great deal that can be done. However, the operation of this tendency, even on a large scale, is only the tip of the iceberg, for it is further reinforced by the profit motive where a commercial venture is in question. There is a constant pressure on firms to increase profits by cutting costs, and to cut costs by cutting corners. What if anything can be done about this? Better and broader consumer protection would be one kind of answer: consumer-protection machinery, especially when enshrined in law, has enjoyed a modest degree of success in recent years. Better still would be effective means for limiting and controling harmful or undesirable manifestations of competitiveness, rather than merely attempting halfheartedly to ameliorate its effects. This will be discussed further in chapter 10, and I will now look at another side of "dehumanization."

The Computer as Decision-Maker

The concern of some people regarding the take-over of everyday tasks by machines runs deeper than simply concern at having to deal with machines and not with people, or being forced to do things in a way which seems geared to the machine and not to the consumer. Anxiety has been expressed in recent years about the way we are being encouraged to look on computers as potential decision-makers. It must be made clear what is meant by this. A machine such as a computer is constantly "taking decisions" in the sense that it is coming to conclusions, that is, producing results about things, given a set of input data. However, these results are looked at by human beings, possibly checked, at least in part, and put into practice by human beings. For a machine really to count as making a decision it must be entrusted with a judgment which will not merely act as a background against which humans can do their decision-making, but which will automatically be implemented. This need not mean that it cannot be revoked by a human operator, only that the computer's decision will routinely pass directly into practice, as opposed to being itself used as a reason by a human being.

There are some kinds of judgments which we would all be happy about entrusting to a machine. We do not, for example, feel threatened by the fact that a computer "decides" when to operate sprinklers according to the temperature, or even that computers should determine the path of aircraft. The point at which people tend to become alarmed is where it seems as though a piece of machinery is making decisions which involve matters of principle and questions of values. Since machines are not human, we have some reservations about their use in determining such things as the proper treatment of human beings, what care they should receive (for example in medicine), how goods should be shared out (economics), and so on. Few people would be entirely happy with having a medical decision, such as whether or not to amputate a limb, taken by a computer unaided and unchecked by any human agent.

When we look into the reasons for such reservations, they are, unfortunately, not always as clear as we would like. We saw in chapter 4 that there is nothing especially error-prone about machines, though the errors they make tend to be significant, a machine being unable to distinguish a significant mistake from a trivial one. Yet machines are not inherently incapable of making this distinction. Could it not be that we simply need better-informed machines? Furthermore, if we were to make the possibility of error sufficiently unlikely, would this not outweigh the massiveness of errors when they do happen to occur?

But, some will argue, no machine is actually a human being, and no machine will have the fellow-feeling with and sympathy for human beings that other people have. Joseph Weizenbaum has argued as follows:

> What could be more obvious than the fact that, whatever intelligence a computer can muster, however it may be acquired, it must always and necessarily be absolutely alien to any and all authentic human concerns? The very asking of the question, "What does a judge (or a psychiatrist) know that we cannot tell a computer?" is a monstrous garbled obscenity. That it has to be put into print at all, even for the purpose of exposing its morbidity, is a sign of the madness of our times. Computers can make judicial decisions, computers can make psychiatric judgements . . . . The point is that they ought not [to] be given such tasks. They may even be able to arrive at "correct" decisions in some cases — but always and necessarily on bases no human being should be willing to accept.[2]

Strong stuff. But the last claim (on which the whole seems to rest) is surely less than obvious. From the fact that computers do not have human concerns (are not "humanly concerned") it does not follow that they cannot have human concerns and human values programmed into them. The fact that they do not have them in the same way as human beings do does not entail that they could not be given them at second hand, as it were. This is not to say that this is actually possible, but only that nothing Weizenbaum says makes it impossible.

In opposition to Weizenbaum, James H. Moore has argued for an empirical approach to the question of whether there are some decisions which computers should never be allowed to make. He argues that the question is predominantly one of whether we have good enough reason to trust the technology to take the decisions in question, and that this must be discovered through the normal methods of experience and research. While agreeing that computers should not be allowed to make decisions about basic goals and values (a condition to which nearly anyone would assent), Moore points out that

> it is at least conceivable that the computer might give outstanding justifications for its decisions ranging from detailed legal precedents to a superb philosophical theory of justice or from instructive clinical observations to an improved theory of mental illness so that the competence of the computer in such decision making was considered to be as good or better than the competence of human experts. Empirically this may never happen but it is not a necessary truth that it will not.[3]

Moore concludes that "some of the most humanistic decisions may well come from decision makers which are not human."

Yet, while Moore's position is in some ways more sophisticated than that of Weizenbaum, it is not without its drawbacks. If (a big "if") human values could in some way be inculcated into machines, there still remains a problem concerning how we would know, or even have satisfactory evidence, that this goal had been fully achieved. What would count as such evidence? Here I am thinking of machines supposedly programmed to act in accordance with human values, not machines which are supposed to have a hand in shaping the values. In the case of a human being we know that he or she, simply by being human, can be relied on to share certain values and responses with us. This occasionally breaks down, as in the case of psychopaths, yet it is a reliable enough assumption to warrant our staking our lives on it. But in the case of a machine the presumption lies in the opposite direction: the onus is surely on the person who wants to make a case for its having the full repertoire of human concerns, values, priorities, and so forth, and not on the person who is skeptical of this claim.

This is especially true if we consider that there is something open-ended about the range of characteristically human responses. This does not mean that there are no such things as human nature, human values, and so on, nor that human nature is infinitely pliable. Rather, it is to recognize that our moral responses are not determined according to rigid codes or strict formulae. They are not merely the result of deductive reasoning from premises, nor simply inferences from observation. All of these things might enter into our decision-making, and yet they do not add up to the kind of practical wisdom which enables us to get our moral lives in order. If this is true, it is bad news for the idea that there could be such a thing as programming a machine to embody this kind of wisdom.

It looks, then, as though there might be good conceptual reasons (though not quite those suggested by Weizenbaum) for thinking that there are at least some kinds of decision on which we should be reluctant to give the last word to a computer. The difficulty lies in identifying the kinds of decision which will fall into this category. We might, for example, wish to say that all decisions of a "moral" character should be in the hands of human beings. However, this moves us little farther, for there is a sense in which all decisions are in some way moral decisions: a decision to do anything at all can, under the right circumstances, be influenced by moral reasons for or against the course of action in question. Often, of course, these moral factors will be relatively trivial and may not significantly affect the balance of pros and cons. This means that there are some decisions in which the moral component is so minimal that we should have no hesitation about letting the final decision be taken by an automaton. The kinds of decision which we have in mind when we talk about the need for invoking distinctively human values are important moral decisions — ones which have effects on the well-being of human beings or other sentient creatures. It is possible that this criterion could be sharpened up more, but unlikely that it could be made completely determinate and watertight. This ought not to worry us very much, however, since the question of what constitutes an important moral decision is itself a moral decision, and we have seen that moral deliberation is not like a precise science, but more like a practical skill, manifesting itself not so much in neat rules and principles as in practice.

Machines and Moral Responsibility

At the bottom of the worry concerning computers as decision makers, then, is the fact that they do not embody human values, priorities, and the like. They may have such features built into them artificially, but no guarantee is possible that their ethical responses would always be consistent with the actions of a mature human being. We are a long way from being able to construct machines which could embody values in this way, and we may well never come close to it at all.

However, even if we succeeded in building and programming a system incorporating human moral values to a very high degree, there would still be something missing. Would not the machine be simply simulating, rather than genuinely embodying, as we do, such values? Unless our techniques in artificial intelligence can make a dramatic leap, not just in degree but in kind, this will be true. It is one thing to build a machine which can act as though certain things matter to it, but quite another to construct a machine to which anything actually does genuinely matter, the way things matter to us.

The feature which is (rightly though perhaps vaguely) seen by people as lacking in machines, and which makes them inappropriate as decision makers in some important cases, could be described as that of moral responsibility. A thing which incorporates the requisites for moral decision-making, but only as simulation without genuine moral concern, cannot be said to be a candidate for bearing moral responsibility: it could not be praised, blamed, or held responsible for any of its actions in the way in which human beings can. Why should this worry us? Is it simply a psychological urge to have somewhere to locate the blame if things go badly wrong which makes us distrust the idea of important decisions being made by even a very good simulation of a moral agent? These questions await a rather fuller discussion of machines as moral agents, in chapter 9.

8. Ownership, Rights, and Information

I suggested in chapter 6 that, regarding information about a person, an important principle ought to be that the contents and whereabouts of the information should be known, or at least knowable, to the person in question. This notion forms one of the main planks of most data-protection legislation. This chapter will be devoted to issues concerning rights over information, especially property rights.

Owning One's Image

An individual is often rightly concerned on discovering that widespread computerized information exists about him or her. As noted in chapter 5, such a person may feel that this in some way violates his or her personality in a deep and disturbing way. A person may respond by claiming sole rights over the existence and transmission of such information ("privacy as control"). Yet it was pointed out that to claim such a blanket right is simply unrealistic: no one can have complete control over what is known about him or her by others, or over the way in which this information may be passed from one source to another. Such a right has never existed before or since the advent of the data bank. The most that can be insisted upon is the right to expect that principles such as those outlined in chapter 6 should be respected. Why, then, the initial reaction of indignation at the very existence of such information, especially when stored in the form of electronic data?

The answer lies in the fact that we somehow feel not only that we have certain rights over, but actually *possess*, the information in question: that we are the owners of our own image, the image stored in the file. It ought to be obvious that there is something odd about the use of the concept of ownership in this context. Information considered simply as such is by no means the kind of thing that can be owned, though as we shall see it can sometimes be bought and sold. Even if it can be owned, this does not constitute a reason for thinking that all information about an individual is necessarily the property of that individual. Yet it is easier to see that there is something wrong with the notion than to see where its initial plausibility lies. I will suggest that the superficial attraction arises from certain features of our intellectual heritage that encourage us to interpret rights over things as ownership, to lean always toward construing rights as property rights. This theme will be taken up later in greater detail, and I move now to consider some other aspects of ownership in connection with information and the technology which stores and processes it.

Commercial Ownership of Data

People's feelings of "owning" the totality of personal data about themselves is not the only problematic issue with regard to the ownership of information. As we have seen already, information is often the subject of business transactions: it is bought and sold like ordinary tangible commodities. We have seen how commercial enterprises will sell lists of names and addresses as advertising targets, records of credit histories, and other personal information on individuals. Any information which may be gathered by one agency and used by another is a possible subject of such transactions, and especially information stored by electronic means and thereby capable of being easily transferable from the files of one person to those of another.

Yet in this kind of case, we still do not appear to be talking about the kind of information or data which can properly be said to be *owned* by someone. If I do not really own all the information about myself which others might have on record, similarly neither do they. And this will apply even if they have "bought" the information from elsewhere, which underlines the fact that the possibility of something's being bought and sold does not entail the possibility of its being owned in the full sense. (Another example is that one can "buy" stolen goods although this does not make one the owner of them.) This seems to be borne out in the attitude of the law in most countries to information of this type. Naturally the possibility exists that someone may acquire lists of names and addresses, for instance, by dishonest means, e.g., by fraud, by breaking and entering, by illicit use of facilities, and so forth. Still, the wrong which has been done lies in the means by which the information was acquired, and not by the very fact of its being acquired and (very possibly) used. Provided the acquisition itself did not contravene any independent moral or legal principles, the issue is only one of data security, that is, how to prevent people from getting hold of it, and this is not a moral but a technical issue. It is possible that it concerns the ethics and law of trade secrecy, if it does not involve any other principle; but trade secrecy is a somewhat nebulous area, as I note later. Where the reproduction and use of information acquired from another source really does become a moral and social problem in its own right is where the information in question is of a technological nature. Here we move into a different area of information ownership: one which concerns not merely the content of the information (names and addresses and so on) contained in data banks and in computers, but the ownership of the very items of software, that is, the programs, which run such systems. This applies to all computer software, whether it is concerned with personal information storage or with anything else, such as industrial processes, research methods, or weapon systems. The difficulties in this area are notorious, and it is to these that I turn before returning to the more general issues of ownership.

The Ownership of Software

When a person writes a computer program, especially if it is intended as a business venture which will benefit that person or the organization for which he or she works, the last thing intended is that someone else will be able to obtain access to it and reap the rewards without the effort. That someone should be able to do so seems, moreover, to be a moral as much as a commercial anathema.

Yet this also is not without its conceptual problems. What, we may ask, is the nature of the right which programmers have over their programs? Is it a right of ownership? And if so, what exactly is it that is owned: the idea itself, the way of expressing it in a given language, the concrete form of it on paper or in a machine's memory, or what? One thing which makes this issue particularly thorny is the lack of agreement within the field on the question of what exactly a computer program *is*. This may sound strange, for most of us have a pretty good idea what a program is: it is the set of instructions which causes a machine to perform a particular sequence of operations. However, consider the following situation. Suppose that I write a program in one programming language which some other person subsequently translates into a different language, and possibly markets. Is what the other person markets the same program as mine? One's first reaction might be to say that it clearly is the same program, since all that the competitor has done is to take what I wrote and translate it. To deny that it is the same program would be like allowing someone to get away with translating *War and Peace* into English and then claiming that it was not the novel written by Tolstoy since Tolstoy's was in Russian. But before drawing such a straightforward conclusion, ask first of all what brings it about that these are instances of plagiarism. Is it merely that one version means the same as the other? It can't be quite this, since two persons could independently come up with writings which were identical in content, without one having plagiarized the writing of the other. In the case of a novel such as *War and Peace*, the chances of this happening are so indescribably remote that we would never believe it to be the case: the only real possibility of duplication is through copying or translating. The same is not the case, however, with computer programs. It is quite possible that, given a specific task to be performed in a given programming language, two programmers will come up with independent programs which are very similar. The simpler the task, the more likely this will be. What is more, there will often be an obvious or optimum way of going about the task which is hit on by both programmers. But have we not now stumbled on a real distinction of principle between what the novelist is doing and what the programmer is up to? It begins to look as though the programmer is expected not to apply his creativity to invent something which is then in some sense his own, but to discover something which was already there to be discovered: something which is independent of any given programming language.

In computing circles such a thing is known as an *algorithm*. An algorithm is, according to the Oxford *Dictionary of Computing*, "A prescribed set of well-defined rules or instructions for the solution of a problem, e.g. the performance of a calculation, in a finite number of steps."

An algorithm is not the program itself but the theoretical sequence of steps which is exemplified in the program, but which could just as easily have been exemplified in a host of other, different programs. It is "the mathematics behind" the program in question. Here an example may be of use. The following two simple programs are written in different computer languages, yet they do the same thing and in the same way. (For anyone not familiar with computer languages, they will be explained in just a moment.) The first is the language FORTRAN 77:

```
PROGRAM ONE
NUM1 = 0
PRINT*, 'ENTER A NUMBER'
```

```
READ*, NUM2
DO 10 N = 1, NUM2
```

```
10      IF (N * N .EQ. NUM2) NUM1 = N
        IF (NUM1 .NE. 0) PRINT*, 'WHOLE SQUARE ROOT IS',
        NUM1
        IF (NUM1 .EQ. 0) PRINT*, 'NO WHOLE SQUARE ROOT'
        STOP
        END
```

The second is in the language PASCAL:

```
PROGRAM Two;
VAR Num1, Num2, i: INTEGER;
BEGIN
    Num1 := 0;
    Writeln ('Enter a number');
    Read(Num2);
    FOR i := 1 TO Num2 DO
            BEGIN
                    IF i * i = Num2 THEN Num1 := i
            END:
    IF Num1 <> 0 THEN Writeln ('Whole square root is', Num1)
            ELSE Writeln ('No whole square root')
END
```

Both programs discover whether a given number (the input, entered by the user) has a square root which is a whole number, and if it does they tell us what it is.[1]

To see how it is that they both do it in the same way we must look at their operation in a little detail. The first program begins with its name (PROGRAM ONE), and then on the second line defines a variable (something which can take different values) called NUM1, giving it, for the time being, the value 0. It then tells the machine to print out the message ENTER A NUMBER to the user. The next line reads in the number entered by the user, and calls it NUM2. The next line is more complicated. It tells the machine to DO everything it finds up to and including the line with the label 10, and to do it for each value of N from 1 to NUM2. (Thus if the NUM2 we put in happened to be 5, it would do it five times, with N taking successively the values 1, 2, 3, 4, and 5.) The following line is itself the line with the label 10, and this says that IF the current value of N is such that N times N equals NUM2 (the number the user entered), then NUM1 (which was originally set to 0) is to be given the current value of N. The next two lines tell the machine that if NUM1 now has a non-zero value (i.e. if it found a whole square root) to print it out with a message, or, if NUM1 still takes the value 0 (i.e., if it didn't find a whole square root), to write out a message to that effect. The instruction STOP tells the machine that it is to stop at this point, and the final line END tells it that there are no further instructions.

In the second program the first line is likewise the name of the program (though PASCAL, unlike FORTRAN, is quite happy with either upper- or lower-case letters). The second line, however, states that we will be using the variables Num1, Num2, and i. In PASCAL these must be declared at the start, whereas in FORTRAN we can bring them into being as we go along. The third line says explicitly that this is the beginning of the program proper. As in the first program the variable Num1 is then given the value 0, though using a different sign to do it. The next line likewise tells the machine to ask for a number, and the one after tells it to read in the number. The line beginning FOR tells it to do everything between the next BEGIN and END, and to do it for every value of i from 1 to Num2 (this is the equivalent of the DO instruction in the first program). What is between the BEGIN and the END is the instruction that if i times i is equal to the number Num2 which we fed in, then NUM1 is to be given the value of i (which is the equivalent of the instruction with the label 10 in the first program). Then the machine is again instructed that if Num1 is non-zero (i. e., a whole square root has been found) it is to write it out with a message, or ELSE to give the message that there is no whole square root. Finally END. tells the machine that this is the finish.

The two programs look different and are, in a sense, different. They are written in different languages, and the devices used in those languages vary somewhat. Yet anyone who has followed the above ought to spot the underlying similarity. We could describe what is done by both programs in exactly the same way. This is not just to say that we could describe them both by saying that they work out whether a given number has a whole square root or not and write it out if it has. Rather, *how* they each do it can be described in the same way. For example: a first variable is given the value zero; a prompt is given for a number to be entered; the entered number is read in as a second variable; each whole number from one to the value of the second variable is then inspected, and if, when multiplied by itself, it yields the same value as that of the second variable, this value is assigned to the first variable, replacing the value one; if the first variable ends up with a non-zero value, that value is written out as the whole square root of the second variable, but if it is still zero, a message is given that there is no whole square root.

This describes neither of the two programs as such, but the algorithm, which is independent of any program and is neutral between all the (infinite number of) programs which could embody it. Thus, in discovering a general method of carrying out a specific task, the programmer may be said to have invented not a program, but an algorithm which could be implemented in an indefinite number of programs. This presents us with an acute problem. For, while an individual program might possibly be said to be the preserve of a particular programmer (nobody else has written precisely this program), the algorithm is a different matter: other, independently developed programs will very possibly be embodiments of the same algorithm. Indeed, it may have been a misnomer when we talked above about "inventing" an algorithm. If an algorithm is a mathematical method, is it not less like an invention than like a law of nature — not invented, like a machine, or composed, like a novel, but *discovered*, like the laws of gravity or the principle of relativity? Clearly the dividing lines between these things are not sharp, but one must be aware that there are such lines.

I have looked at three ways in which the question of ownership of, and rights over, computer-held information might arise. Generally speaking, the legal position concerning the problems discussed in this book will be left until the last chapter. However, as in the case of data protection I will have to jump the gun a little by looking briefly at the attitude of the law to the issue in hand. It is difficult, if not impossible, to avoid legal questions when discussing property and ownership, since they are at least partly legal concepts.[2]

The Current Position

The three relevant areas of the law which need to be considered are the law of *trade secrets*, the law of *copyright*, and the law regarding *patent*. I take these separately.

Trade secrets. As we saw above this is one way in which both data and programs can be protected in law. The law of trade secrets is a matter of common law, not statute law. That is to say, it is not created by the passing of bills in Parliament, but is decided by the courts on the basis of custom, reason, and precedents set by other relevant decisions. The basis on which trade secrets law is meant to rest is not explicitly laid down anywhere, and as a result it has been a matter of dispute among lawyers and students of jurisprudence. One kind of argument which can be used in bringing a case under trade secrets law is that the secret involved was the property of the person or the company from whom it was "stolen." Another, which may be used where a trade secret has been divulged by an employee (as is often the case), is that an explicit or implicit contract committed the employee to keeping the secret. Thirdly, the concept of confidence can be invoked regarding the divulging of a secret or a breach of confidence of a kind for which legal redress can be sought. It has been demonstrated recently that there is something to be said for each of these three approaches as a foundation for the law of trade secrets. It has even been suggested that in some sense all three ingredients are present, in different measures, wherever a trade secret has been "stolen" or dishonestly given away. Two things, however, suggest otherwise. One is the tenuous character of the argument that an implicit contract can bind a person not to divulge a secret. It seems to create the possibility of someone being penalized for doing something which is not illegal in itself and which that person never agreed not to do; but it is also unclear how the notion of a non-explicit contract can avoid collapsing into that of a breach of confidentiality. The second is the general problem of talking about secrets as property.

When we talk about property in everyday life we usually have in mind something tangible, which can be bought and sold in the simple sense of being handed over by one person to another person, who can pick it up and take it away. However, most of us are probably vaguely aware that there are other kinds of property, such as companies, land, and money which exist only on paper. When we begin to scratch the surface, the concept of property turns out to be not at all as simple as it seems at first sight. Not only are there all these different kinds of property, but each of them seems to be property in a slightly different sense and to obey its own rules, for example, regarding what kinds of rights are involved in owning the thing in question. This presents problems for anyone who wishes to lump all these cases together as simply cases of "ownership" *tout court*. Where the thing supposedly owned is a piece of information, this problem is especially acute, for it is not certain in what "the piece of information" consists. As we saw above this is equally true in the case of a program or method of solving a problem. All the obvious ways of answering the question seem equally implausible. Is the thing owned to be thought of as being the physical embodiment which it has been given by the owner? In other words, suppose I have a trade secret which consists of the discovery that cars will run on lemonade. Is the secret that I own simply the piece of paper with the words "Cars will run on lemonade" written on it? This cannot be the case, for we already have a perfectly good law which says that one must not steal pieces of paper, or for that matter any other physical objects, from another person. Its constituting a trade secret would be irrelevant. But if what is owned is not to be thought of as the physical embodiment, is it then to be considered as somehow the information itself, that is, the content of the secret, or, to put it another way, "the facts"? Unfortunately this looks equally odd. What could it mean to say that I own a fact? It may well be that if I am the first to discover a particular fact I have a claim to a special share of the benefit that accrues from the knowledge. But this does not add up to ownership. If a fact such as the information that cars will run on lemonade could be said to be someone's property, what about the fact that Ben Nevis is 4,406 feet high, or that the earth rotates on its axis? Here we seem to have lost all grip on the concept of property. Even such things as Boyle's Law and Fleming's Left-Hand Rule are not thought of as being the property of the gentlemen in question. For these and similar reasons lawyers both in Britain and the United States have fought shy of basing the law of trade secrets on the idea of secrets as property. Lord Denning in 1969 rather characteristically stated, "The jurisdiction is based not so much on property or on contract as on the duty to be of good faith."[3] Much earlier, in the United States, Mr. Justice Holmes had observed that

> the word "property" as applied to trademarks and trade secrets is an unanalysed expression of certain secondary consequences of the primary fact that the law makes some rudimentary requirements of good faith. . . . The property may be denied but the confidence cannot be. Therefore the starting point for the present matter is not property.[4]

Why, given all these considerations, should many people nevertheless wish to regard secrets as property, something which can be owned in the literal sense? We will leave this question until we have looked at the other two areas of law which are relevant to our concerns.

Copyright. The law of copyright, as applied to data stored in retrieval systems such as computer data bases, applies only where the information is itself the subject of copyright, that is, would be protected by copyright independently of whether or not it were stored in this form.

With regard to copyright, the law differs somewhat in Britain and the United States, in that for material to be protected by copyright in the United States it must be both published and registered as copyright, whereas these two conditions do not apply in the United Kingdom. What the copyright laws of both countries have in common, however, is that, as they stand in statute, they are ambiguous as to whether they apply to computer programs or not, though both apply to data. Here again we run into the conceptual problem of defining where the program, the software, resides. If we say that it is the actual program as written and stored in the machine, someone could easily make a "copy" which is sufficiently different from the original not to count; or could simply render the same algorithm in a different programming language and call it a different program. This is partly a result of the fact that copyright laws tend to talk quite freely about "copying" or "copies," without making it clear what is supposed to constitute a copy. This also presents a problem (both in the case of programs and of data) when we ask whether the storing of some text on a magnetic disk or tape constitutes copying it. Obviously if I record someone else's material from that person's disk onto my own and then print it out on paper, the paper version is a copy: but is the magnetic version a copy? Remember that it consists of nothing but magnetized or unmagnetized segments of a disk or tape. Could such a thing constitute a copy, say, of *War and Peace*? And if so, in what sense? A similar problem arises in the case of a machine-readable form of a program. As we know, a program written in one of the ordinary programming languages cannot be read by the computer until it is translated by a device called a compiler into a macnine-readable form known as the "object program," as opposed to the original "source program." Does the object program constitute a copy of the source program or not? On the one hand, one's initial reaction is probably that the person who has the rights over the source program should have similar rights also over its machine-readable form. On the other hand, however, the object program cannot be protected by copyright, since it will vary from machine to machine (a version readable by one machine will not be readable by another); nor is it entirely clear that a translation as such is a copy.

Patent. When we look at the law regarding patent, both in Britain and the United States, we find problems analogous to those which we saw in the case of trade secrets and of copyright. Here the question of the protection of data does not arise (patents exist to protect not information, but inventions or techniques) but obviously that of programs does.

While it is generally agreed that programs, under some conditions, can be patented, there is a lack of agreement about what these conditions are. Once again this disagreement turns on the question of where the program actually resides: in the exact form of it produced by the programmer, or in the algorithm which the program expresses? Most commentators agree that a pure algorithm cannot be the subject of a patent. For example, the simple method I described of finding a whole square root could not be patented, since it is not the sort of thing which is "invented," but the sort of thing which is "discovered." But the question of where we draw the line between patentable and non-patentable material depends upon being able to sharpen the intuititive distinction between the inventable and the merely discoverable.

One approach is to say that inventions constitute knowledge of how to do something, whereas discoveries embody knowledge that something is the case. However, we saw in chapter 2, when discussing the distinction between science and technology, that this distinction will not bear a great deal of weight, since many, perhaps all, cases of knowing *how* can be construed as cases of knowing *that*, and vice versa.

An alternative approach would be to claim that a merely discoverable fact (the height of Ben Nevis, for example) is something which in the long run would have been discovered by someone else, had not the actual discoverer done so, whereas an invention is something which, if it had not been thought of by its actual inventor, would not have been thought of at all. This distinction, however, is equally shaky, since it depends so heavily on unverifiable counterfactuals (statements about what would have been the case were things different in some way from how they are).

It may appear that we are unlikely to frame effective laws which will capture exactly what we want in protecting data and software from piracy and the like. However, this need not be as a result of something especially awkward or essentially unmanageable about the artifacts of data technology. It may be that there is something wrong in what we want: that is, it could be that we began with the wrong expectations. In order to show what I mean by this, I return now to the idea of ownership in general.

The Concept of Ownership

Many of the difficulties encountered in talking about rights over information spring from the concepts of property and ownership, the different ways in which they are understood, and the degree of reliance ordinarily placed on them. Before going further, it will be wise to point to a distinction between the way in which these terms are used in ordinary discourse and in law. In everyday speech, we regard as synonymous the expressions "I own x" and "x is my property." In strict legal parlance, however, goods can indeed be *owned*, but (and here is the apparent paradox) they cannot be *property*; the only things which can count as property are *rights*, where these are rights over things, that is, over goods, and among these rights over things is the right of ownership. Thus, strictly speaking, to own something is to have the property right of ownership over it.[5] While, on the one hand, this fulfils the function of reminding us that ownership is not the only way of having rights over something, on the other hand, it may tend to obscure the fact that ownership itself is nothing more than a bundle of rights. The reason why this fact is so easy to obscure is because of the widespread but misguided idea that the right of ownership is some kind of absolute, monolithic right — a right to do whatever one likes with the thing owned. That this is not so is obvious from only a little reflection: the fact that this penknife belongs to me does not mean that I can stick it in someone with impunity. Naturally the defender of the absolutist view will try to reformulate it in ways such as "do whatever one likes *to* the thing," as opposed to "*with* the thing," or "do whatever one likes which doesn't harm other people." None of these will stand up, however. The first distinction, for example, is impossible to formulate clearly; and the second (like John Stuart Mill's distinction between self-regarding and other-regarding actions, which it closely resembles) easily collapses when we consider that even the most innocent use of my own property may harm somebody, for example, by giving offense. What is needed is not a tighter formulation of what it is to own something, as opposed to merely having certain rights over it, but *less insistence on the idea of ownership in the first place*. Once we accept that ownership is no more than a bundle of rights of certain kinds (which will vary depending on the kind of thing owned, and probably on many other factors), we may feel less need to place so much emphasis on the concept of ownership at the expense of rights or claims of other kinds.

What is more, when we cease concentrating exclusively, or almost exclusively, on ownership, we see that the situation which we have been discussing so far in this chapter does not appear in as bad a light as it seemed above. The question from which we began, concerning whether or not information can be regarded as property, need not arise.

That is, we will no longer feel the need to answer the question one way or the other, and therefore will not end up being caught in an impossible fork. As a result the legal solution of granting rights which are not rights of ownership, and granting them on the merits of each case, begins to look like a sensible procedure and not a ragged and ad hoc expedient.

What we have seen is a tendency to construe rights over things as ownership rights wherever possible, a tendency to insist on asking not "What rights, if any, do I have concerning this or that thing?", but "Do I *own* it or not?" We have seen that this exists in the three areas of personal information about oneself, commercially held data, and software. In all three cases this has been found not to be a fruitful approach. With regard to personal information concerning oneself, it seems to make more sense to talk in terms of rights to know what such information exists, to have access to it, and to amend it where it is incorrect. In the case of data which is commercially stored, the only rights which can seriously be upheld are those which protect one from having this data pirated by means which themselves are illegal for independent reasons. And with software, trade secrets, copyright, and patent turn out to be more useful concepts than that of ownership. Why, then, do we find that individuals and organizations display this fondness for the notion of ownership as the pivot of their claims?

I suggested earlier that we live in a culture which embodies and encourages a preoccupation with ownership and a propensity to see it as something simple and monolithic — a very special kind of relation between a person (or group of people) and the thing owned. I also argued that no blanket statement of what ownership consists of is going to be plausible if it is supposed to be applicable to all kinds of ownable things and in all circumstances. Yet this is not to say that there is nothing at all in the concept of ownership; much less is it to suggest that we ought to stop operating with the notion altogether. Rather, it will be more instructive to examine how the concept has developed into the central notion in the field of rights, where extravagant and out-of-place ownership claims can be made to look at least superficially plausible.

A Widening Circle

It is reasonable to suppose that the earliest, and conceptually the simplest, form of ownership is that in which an individual is recognized as having a special kind of claim over a small number of moderately sized items for which he or she has a regular and legitimate use. These may, for example, include clothes, tools, cooking utensils, furniture, and the like. The anthropological evidence indicates that primitive tribal societies limit individual ownership to such items, and rest ownership of more important goods, including land, in the community as a whole. In some other kinds of primitive societies it is not the tribe but the extended family which forms the most important social unit; but the pattern of ownership seems to follow similar lines, individual ownership being limited to minor chattels, with the head of the family having the management (though not, in any normal sense, the ownership) of major items such as the dwelling house.[6] Furthermore, rights exist in primitive societies which are not ownership rights (for example, grazing rights), though it is unlikely that the rights themselves are regarded by the participants as property as we might understand it.

Individual ownership of larger and more abstract objects seems to come later, being both historically and conceptually less primitive than the ownership of simple chattels. In varying degrees we might include here private ownership of land, herds, businesses, money, stocks and shares, and even other human beings as slaves. But besides a development in the *kind* of things which can be owned, the concept seems to have undergone another change during its history with regard to ideas about the *extent* of legitimate ownership. For while primitive man no doubt laid claim to the ownership of the objects of his regular use — the familiar objects which made up his circumscribed personal world, and the ownership of which distinguished him from the rest of his group — modern man (if he is lucky) may own not only money which he has done nothing to earn, but land which he has never seen, property on which he has never set foot, and controling interests in businesses about which he knows nothing — even including the fact that he owns them. It is reasonable to argue that these massive changes of degree actually add up to a qualitative change in the concept of ownership: once the circle which encompasses that which may be privately owned has expanded to such a degree, we are no longer talking about the same thing as the primitive person laying claim to a small stock of personal effects.

The difference seems to reside, largely, in the way in which ownership is justified or established (justified in general, or established in particular cases). In a primitive society the idea of ownership involves a moral right based on possession and use, usually with some rudimentary legal machinery for deciding disputed cases. In more complex societies, however, ownership has become almost entirely a legal concept. Whether someone has the right of ownership over a thing has thus become almost wholly divorced from the question of moral rights, such as the right to the means of one's livelihood, and is now primarily to do with the way in which something has been bought and sold.

This difference seems to be mirrored in the dichotomy between the two chief modern theories concerning the justification of private ownership in general: appropriationism and contractualism.[7] The former, as expounded by Locke, Kant, and, more recently, Robert Nozick, tends to rest the case for ownership on the supposed original appropriation of unowned goods in a primal state of nature, while the latter places the emphasis on the so-called social contract and on the notion of a contractual agreement as such. The appropriationist view seems to have more in common with the idea of ownership as pertaining primarily to personal effects made "one's own" by use and habit, and the contractualist position allies itself more naturally with the understanding of ownership which is rooted in commercial transaction. The philosophical battle between these two schools of thought, which has been waged sporadically since the seventeenth century, may be seen as the attempt to hold together a concept which in practice has bifurcated in response to shifting economic patterns.

The existence of these philosophical traditions should also remind us that the trends which we are discussing are not of very recent origin. The possibilities of a person or small group owning vast tracts of land, international businesses, and so on, although perhaps on a smaller scale, goes back many hundreds of years, as does the idea of the right of private ownership as somehow the paradigm of what a right should be. The important point here is that the habits of thought which this bloated and over-exalted concept has encouraged have become a hindrance. This is the case especially when a new set of questions, such as those concerning information, data, and software, presents itself. The fixation of Western societies on the idea of private ownership, together with the assumption that virtually anything which can be the object of a right can be the object of an ownership right, tends to make us ask the wrong questions in the first place. Instead of trying to throw light on particular sorts of cases, inquiring what rights or claims different parties might reasonably be judged to have over a given resource, the first questions which often occur are, "Who owns it?" "Do I?" "Do we?" "If not, can we bring it about that we own it?" And so on. It remains the case, as we have seen, that broader and richer ideas regarding ownership and its relation with other kinds of rights are embodied in our legal systems, if only vestigially. Yet it cannot be certain that these will meet the challenges of the future. Our present ways of talking and thinking about such matters have developed from the relatively uncomplicated conceptual apparatus needed by primitive peoples, through the framework of law and custom which characterized feudal society, to the kind of monolithic structure required by the capitalist state, with its glorification of acquisition and its apotheosis of private ownership. It is always dangerous to predict the future and the kinds of response it will demand of us. It should, however, be fairly plain that what the era of information technology will *not* demand from us is a renewed commitment to the centrality of private ownership and the narrowness of outlook which tends to be its concomitant.

9. Moral Attitudes to Machines?

So far I have been discussing questions which concern the effects of computerization and information technology. That is, I have been looking at questions about what our responses should be to the consequences of such technology. To round off this collection of problems it may be worth looking a little at a unique, rather off-beat cluster of issues regarding the potential moral attributes of machines or systems themselves. Although idiosyncratic, these issues are coming to be discussed increasingly in the literature about computers and their social effects — perhaps, as we shall see, a little prematurely. The motivation for such discussion is, on the surface, simple. If information technology and artificial intelligence continue to progress at the current rate, there may be good reason for asking if we might someday find ourselves having to adopt moral attitudes to the artifacts which we ourselves have created.

To begin on a light note, consider this extract from Michael Frayn's novel *The Tin Men*, in which he describes the enthusiasm of a fictional artificial intelligence researcher for just this topic:

> Mackintosh had concentrated all his department's efforts on the Samaritan programme. The simplest and purest form of the ethical situation, as he saw it, was the one in which two people are aboard a raft which would support only one of them, and he was trying to build a machine which would offer a coherent ethical behaviour pattern under these circumstances. It was not easy. His first attempt, Samaritan I, had pushed itself overboard with great alacrity, but it had gone overboard to save anything which happened to be next to it on the raft, from seven stone of lima beans to twelve stone of wet seaweed. After many weeks of stubborn argument Mackintosh had conceded that the lack of discrimination in this response was unsatisfactory, and he had abandoned Samaritan I and developed Samaritan II, which would sacrifice itself only for an organism at least as complicated as itself.[1]

What perhaps amuses us in the above passage is not so much the conviction that what Mackintosh is trying to do is somehow logically or theoretically impossible: most of us probably have no settled views on the issue one way or the other. It is rather Mackintosh's absurd optimism and self-confidence, his ill-thought-out claims for his invention. The fictional example is a good one, partly because in no area of technology do such inflated claims appear in a more ludicrous light than in artificial intelligence, especially where the issue is the building of machines with human attributes such as moral conscience. In this chapter I shall look briefly at the question of whether we ought ever to consider treating some kinds of machines as morally relevant. This has two sides to it. The first is the question of whether machines could ever be properly thought to have moral claims on us, and the second is whether they could ever be properly regarded as moral agents in their own right. Some moral philosophers have regarded these two questions as being very closely connected, to the point of denying that any creature which is not a responsible moral agent can be seen as having rights, that is, claims on others. However, this has the effect — now normally regarded as undesirable — of ruling out animals as having moral claims, and even worse, babies, many of the insane, and the seriously mentally subnormal. Most people therefore consider the class of beings toward which one can have responsibilities as being much wider than the class of beings which can themselves be said to have moral responsibilities, that is, claims on them. Where might "intelligent machines" fit into this scheme of things?

The question arises as a result of the increasing complexity and sophistication of computers and computer systems, a situation which has led some people to suggest that we are even now on the brink of being able to build machines which are actually *alive*. If this is the case, some issues will arise very acutely concerning how we should see our moral relations with the new life form we have created. What will be our moral obligations to these creatures? What, if any, will be their obligations to us? What place will the ideas of trust, affection, friendship, resentment, and other moral concepts play in our interaction with them? In other words how, if at all, will we need to react to them from a moral point of view?

Since the two sides of the issue tend to overlap, no attempt will be made to keep them wholly separate. However, we will begin with the question of moral agency, as being the harder of the two, and consider that of moral claims as it arises.

Criteria of Moral Agency

Could we imagine circumstances in which we would ever be led to admit certain kinds of machines as full members of the "moral community" that we as human beings belong to? The initial problem in answering this question is that philosophers differ in their responses to the question, What is it that makes a creature a moral agent in general? If some kinds of machines, now or in the future, deserve to be thus regarded, they will inevitably be borderline cases, at least in the first place. We have plenty of experience of dealing with borderline cases of moral agency. Few people would wish to regard a new-born baby as a moral agent (though naturally, we have to start treating children as such long before they really are morally responsible, in order to initiate them into the activities that go along with it). At a somewhat later age, however, children can clearly be regarded as morally responsible in some ways, though not in others. Similarly the mentally ill and the mentally subnormal fall into the borderline area when it comes to ascribing moral responsibility.

Traditionally the answers which philosophers have given to the question of what constitutes the criterion for moral agency fall into two categories — though to state it in this way is a great simplification. The first kind of answer is that moral agency is a result of the possession of rationality (this being the supposed reason why human beings can be thought of as moral agents, but not the other animals). A creature is seen as capable of genuine moral responsibility to the extent that it can be seen as rational. The second approach is to locate the source of moral responsibility in some special, or at least sophisticated, kind of emotion or feeling. On this view, a creature will count as a candidate insofar as it is capable of moral feelings. This is a dichotomy (probably misleading, as we shall see) which has been bequeathed to us largely by the philosophers of the eighteenth century. Machines with feelings, in the sense of "sentiments," are a long way in the future, if the possibility can be said to exist at all. But when it comes to reason, is this not surely where computers come into their own? This being so, would not a rationalist (reason-based) account of moral action favor the claim that some machines might be real moral agents?

The point at which the rationalist account has usually run into trouble concerns the fact that it is hard to get from the concept of rationality alone to that of moral understanding. There is some sense in which machines, even the ones we know today, express rationality. Yet, at least on a minimal understanding of what it is to be rational, this cannot be enough on its own. The philosopher David Hume (1711–76) is famous, among other things, for having asserted that "reason alone can never be a motive to any action of the will."[2] But this is to take a deliberately "thin" theory of rationality. What Hume meant by "reason" was no more than "the discovery of truth or falsehood,"[3] which for Hume comes down ultimately to a mere matter of inference and calculation. Immanuel Kant (1724–1804) opposed Hume in proposing to base morality on reason and on reason alone.[4] However, what Kant meant by rationality included more than Hume would have allowed, its chief morally relevant component being, for Kant, a kind of disinterestedness or impartiality which restrains us from doing those things which we would not be able to recommend to everybody. (For example, I cannot rationally assent to a universal practice of telling lies, for if the practice were universal there would be no reason to believe what anybody said, and therefore no advantage to be gained by lying.) Although impressive in its conception, the trouble with Kant's account is that, while it illuminates certain facets of the moral life, it fails to capture everything we would wish to include under this head. An even more comprehensive account of what we might mean by rational might include such things as the capacity to form a humanly intelligible set of priorities, the ability to view things in proportion, to see things in perspective, and the like. Including these kinds of things renders far more promising the idea of including moral deliberation within the sphere of reason. However, we have now got rather far away from the kind of "reason" which machines are celebrated for being good at, their particular *forte* being Hume's kind, which consists merely of ability in logical and calculative manipulation. We have, in fact, entered the area where it is unclear whether we are talking about reasons and rationality or about feelings or emotions. Indeed, in their broadest senses it is difficult to make an unambiguous distinction between the two.

Some Minimum Conditions

Rather than approaching the topic by attempting to answer the question of what constitutes moral agency in general, it may be wiser to think initially about minimum conditions, that is, necessary rather than sufficient conditions. Almost all writers on ethics would agree that a creature suitable to be thought of as a moral agent must: (a) be a *thinking* being, able to deliberate, and (b) possess *free will*. We are now in the position of having to ask: Are the kinds of machines which mankind may be able to build in the future likely to meet these requirements? The first condition presents us immediately with a thorny problem, for the question of whether what machines do is really thinking has been one of the perennial problems — some would say one of the perennial bugbears — of artificial intelligence. To some extent, the furor which this debate has caused has been a result of confusion on the part of the protagonists. On the one hand, those who have designed and built "intelligent" systems have been inclined to say, "Well, the thing can work out any logical or mathematical puzzle you put to it, it can play master standard chess, it composes music and poetry: What more do you want before you will admit that it really thinks?" Philosophers and more reflective computer scientists, on the other hand, have been inclined to give a response such as, "Yes, we know that the thing is in some sense very clever indeed, but it does not follow from this that it is really thinking, as opposed to just behaving as though it were thinking." Thus to the AI (artificial intelligence) people it has often seemed that the philosophers keep shifting the goal by continually saying, "Yes, they may be able to do all that, but they will never be able to do *this*." While to the philosophically minded it has typically appeared that the AI writers have completely ignored the question of whether machine thought is real or merely apparent, and concentrated on giving more elaborate versions of it, as though someone were to answer the charge of forgery by producing bank notes of progressively higher value and saying, "Look, this is a *hundred* — surely you can't suspect *that* of being a dud!"

Philosophers are generally agreed that an integral part of thought is the ability to form and use concepts. That is, the capacity to acquire a mental tool-bag based on the words which make up our language. Words and concepts go together, since, on the one hand, without words we would not be able to acquire shared concepts at all. As the twentieth-century philosopher Ludwig Wittgenstein argued in some of his most famous passages, concepts which are not shared are no concepts at all, for we can assign no determinate meaning to them, or be right or wrong in using them in any given way. And on the other hand, and more trivially, words without concepts would be nothing but empty sounds. Computers certainly use words, at least in some sense or other. What we typically feed into them comes in the form of words, as does that which we get from them. Yet, although the words certainly have a sense from the point of view of the user or programmer of the machine, it is far from obvious that they have any sense at all for the machine itself. If machines really do use words to form concepts which form the content of their thought, what kinds of things can they be said to think *about*? A tempting answer would be to say that they think about whatever the words which they use refer to. If the machine is dealing with a line of input or a chunk of its memory which says "Grass is green," what it is thinking about is grass and greenness. What could be more obvious? But we may then ask: What is it that brings it about that what the machine is thinking about when it uses the word grass, is grass and not, say, jelly? In the case of the programmer there is no difficulty in pointing to what it is that brings this about. The programmer has been taught the use of the word grass by parents or teachers, most likely by means of having it pointed out, that is, by ostensive definition. Human beings do not, it is true, learn all concepts by direct acquaintance with their objects, but it is safe to say that it is direct acquaintance which allows them to grasp to get the primary ones, and that they acquire the others by building on what is primary. A typical computer, however, has no actual experience of grass or of anything else; not just because it is never introduced to anything external, but because it *could not* be — it has no sense organs. Asserting, therefore, that the machine knows something about grass simply on the grounds that it has access to the sentence "Grass is green" is like thinking that we are really giving information about, say, potassium cyanide to a young child by saying to it "potassium cyanide is a toxin." Yet the possibility exists of bringing the child to understand eventually what this sentence means, whereas in the case of the computer there is no way of breaking the circle of ignorance, short of making it capable of learning in a way similar to that in which a child learns. How likely is this latter?

This is a question on which different writers tend to be at variance, owing largely to the infancy of the topic compared with some longer-standing concerns in AI research. As far as the primary requirement — sensory apparatus — is concerned, it is certainly possible to construct a machine which in some sense "sees" and "feels" via sensory transducers. These are merely devices which transform the information in one medium (light rays, contact between surfaces) into information which the machine itself is able to handle, usually in digital electronic form. For a machine to be said to interact with the world in the full sense, however, it must be capable not only of being acted on by the outside world, but also of acting upon it. To this end a machine which could be seen as having a claim to be really thinking — to have anything to think about — would also require motor transducers. These are the opposite of sensory transducers, and convert the processes inside the machine into action, for example, moving objects around. The machine is thus enabled to perform those manipulatory functions which, on a fairly orthodox account of how learning takes place, are essential to elementary concept-formation.

Here arises the issue of machines having moral claims on us. If one imagines a system with a very sophisticated sensory apparatus, it may be suspected that such a system would be sentient and would, for example, feel pain — probably the most morally relevant aspect of sensation. For those who accept that all sentient beings have moral claims, this would seem to settle the issue. Yet this is overly simple. To be sentient does not in itself imply being capable of feeling pain, for two reasons. First, the human sensory apparatus which enables hearing, seeing, and the like is not the same as that which deals with pain. The physiology of pain in human beings is a complex business which is still far from being fully understood. The philosopher Daniel Dennett, in a paper entitled "Why You Can't Make a Computer That Feels Pain," has reservations not only about the completeness of current physiological accounts, but also concerning the consistency of our everyday notion of pain. He talks of a possible "irredeemable incoherency in our ordinary concept of pain," but goes on to explain:

> If and when a good physiological . . . theory of pain is developed, a robot could in principle be constructed to instantiate it. Such advances in science would probably bring in their train wide-scale changes in what we found intuitive about pain, so that the charge that our robot only suffered what we artificially called pain would lose its persuasiveness. In the meantime (if there were a cultural lag) thoughtful people would refrain from kicking such a robot.[5]

Secondly, to imagine a machine equipped with a full set of sensory apparatus is not necessarily to imagine a machine which is actually conscious. The question of consciousness will be discussed shortly; what we must bear in mind here is that there is a sense of "sentient" (i.e., just possessing sense organs or their equivalent) in which it is not clear that a sentient being need be conscious — and only a consciously sentient being could properly be said to have a claim on our moral sympathies.

If we have not settled the issue about consciousness, have we at least settled the issue about thinking? Unfortunately even with the most sophisticated forms of input and output along the above lines most existing machines are very poor candidates for really being able to think, in the full sense in which human beings think. The vast majority, even of AI machines, are non-starters in this respect. Despite all the sensory and motor capacities of present-day robots, their thought capacities do not even begin to approach those of human beings in certain respects. One important feature of human intelligence, for instance, is the ability to recognize an enormous number of complex items very quickly, and from only an apparently small number of "clues." Think, for example, of how we recognize faces or voices. The number of factors which make up the pattern we recognize is huge, and yet recognition is usually instantaneous whenever we have seen a face before for any length of time. What is more, we can even recognize faces when only partially seen, as when all but the region around the eyes is covered up. Think also of how, as very small children, we are able to master a language as complicated as English, and to recognize grammatical constructions immediately, without reference to any explicit rules of grammar.

These sorts of consideration have convinced many researchers that traditional AI approaches have been on the wrong lines as far as the simulation of human thought is concerned. Human thought, it is argued, cannot depend on the capacity to store lots of pieces of discrete information such as "Grass is green." If we could look in somebody's brain we would find no specific "Grass is green" portion of it — nor even a specific "grass" portion. Nor can it depend on the mastery of sets of explicit rules. Rather, it arises out of the ability to learn naturally and "automatically" from our environment. What this might mean we shall see in a moment. For these reasons some recent work in AI has concentrated on the attempt to build systems which might ultimately think and be aware of their environment just as human beings are, because their learning and thinking processes resemble those of human beings. Such systems have, for reasons which will become apparent, come to be known as "connectionist," and it may be worth looking briefly at them before moving on with the discussion.

Machines That Think Like Us?

Behind this new AI technology are a particular model of how the human brain might function and the idea of constructing machines according to the same general pattern in order to try and reproduce in the machines those features of the brain which make us capable of genuine thought. The model of the brain employed in this method is not new, dating back to the late 1940s. Essentially it is the theory that the brain stores its information not so much in the actual brain cells, or neurons, but in the connections between them, and especially in the pattern of relative strengths of connections between cells. According to this view, associative learning and memory is possible chiefly because of a particular feature of brain cell connections: if two cells are active at the same time, the connection between them will be strengthened, thus making it more likely that one will trigger the other in the future. The cluster of methods which aim at reproducing this in artificial systems is called Connectionism. Connectionist methods offer the possibility of a more realistic simulation of human thought by machines.[6]

As noted in chapter 1, at the heart of any computer is a processor, which is what actually performs the tasks presented to the machine. One common machine task is to search through its memory for some item which is to be retrieved. Rather than having a single processor looking at each item in turn, it is possible to construct a machine that has a number of processors working in parallel, performing different parts of the search simultaneously. This is a "parallel architecture." Where the number of processors involved is very large, the type of architecture is "massive parallelism." The possibility of creating machines of this kind attracted initial interest partly as a result of the fact that many physiologists believe the brain's enormous power arises not from having elements powerful in themselves, but from possessing a huge number of simple elements (the neurons) with many interconnections (a single neuron may have up to 10,000 inputs) working in parallel.

Connectionist architectures are a sub-class of massively parallel architectures. The unique feature of the connectionist method is that the items in the machine's memory are not stored in words made up of binary digits, as in a conventional computer memory, but as a pattern of connections between the individual processors, which also act simultaneously in sending their signals. In connectionist architectures the individual processors tend to be extremely simple, and we refer to them as "processing elements," or simply "elements." Often they are capable of nothing more complex than the tasks of: (a) receiving simple incoming signals, (b) performing elementary operations on them, and (c) sending out simple signals over some or all of the other connections. An item in memory is typically represented not within any given processing element, but as a pattern of connections between many elements. This is known as a "distributed representation." Notice that this is totally unlike the idea behind a database, which observes the rule of one fact in one place. This brings it about, among other things, that damage to one single cell or group of cells is not going to destroy a single item of memory (just as the human brain can survive damage without necessary memory loss). The connections between the elements are not merely on/off connections, but can be given different weights, thus rendering the number of possible connection patterns enormously large. It is through selectively altering the weights attached to different connections that the machine is programmed. Strictly speaking, however, such a machine is not programmed, but "learns." A distributed representation, unless it is very simple indeed, will normally be too subtle to be tinkered around with by a programmer, and the development of the machine's memory must inevitably proceed by means of automatic learning and not by conscious human adjustment. Moreover, it is demonstrably possible to build machines whose learning abilities include the capacity for correcting or adjusting parts of memory throughout the system in the light of new acquisitions. Architectures have already been designed which incorporate semantic networks, embodying relationships between different concepts. There is good evidence that machines with this type of organization can be made to recognize and learn from visual patterns, and also to recognize, to a certain extent, human speech. The scale on which connectionist architectures are being conceived is constantly on the increase, with some researchers now talking about a machine containing a million or more processors. Whether or not these methods do turn out to be the key to building machines with human-like thought capacities remains to be seen. We have, so far, hardly witnessed the opening stages of their development. If they do, however, it is possible that their progressive elaboration might one day lead us into moral difficulties of the kinds described earlier. Before concluding anything quite so alarming, however, let me examine whether the anticipated advances are such as to tempt us to take machines seriously as moral agents.

Consciousness and Moral Agency

I began by asking whether machines could ever be said to think as human beings do, and so far I have been content to let this mean something like: Could they have capacities which approximate to those of human beings? It is not entirely clear, however, that I have not simply done what was warned against above, and shown that it is possible, in principle, to simulate human thought to a very high degree, but *only to simulate* it. What more could we possibly ask for, in seeking an example of a machine with a claim to be treated as a moral agent? An obvious feature, though by no means an easy one to deal with, is *consciousness*. If we could satisfy ourselves of the possibility of building a machine which possesses consciousness, this would have two major consequences for the present topic. First, it would show how such machines could ever have a moral claim on us. If we were convinced that the machines we created were really aware of what we were doing to them, and could really feel, as opposed to merely possessing some feeling-type apparatus, and really suffer, this would raise obvious problems for us in our relations with them. As one recent writer has expressed it:

> When a machine is useless, too old or malfunctioning in some way, we simply destroy it with no regrets. But what are the ethics of destroying, when it suits us and just because it suits us, a thinking, conscious machine that may or may not be aware of our intentions? And what do we do if the machine begs us not to destroy it?[7]

Secondly, the notion of consciousness can offer a way into the second of the two conditions from which I began this section of the discussion — the condition of free will. The philosophical literature on the question of free will is enormous. Some would deny that a machine could act freely simply because it is deterministic; what happens within it is just what has to happen according to the laws of physics. Other people would point to the fact that a computer is programmed, claiming that anything which is "merely" obeying a set of instructions in this way cannot be acting from free choice. The trouble with both of these points is that similar things can be said of human beings. People are physical organisms which obey the laws of physics as much as does anything else in the universe. Factors in the physical and psychological make-up of human beings are analogous to programming: people have genetic codes, social conditioning and background, and so on. The attempt to explain what makes us different from machines is to talk about a soul, as something separate from the body, standing to the body as a driver does to a vehicle, taking the real decisions and taking them freely. This conception goes back at least to Plato and is still perpetuated in at least some popular religion. The drawback of this claim, however, is that it seems not to be capable of being substantiated, either by reason or observation. If there can be said to be a consensus among modern philosophers regarding the issue of free will, it is probably something like the following. Human beings are physical creatures whose bodies obey the laws of physics. Yet our own experience tells us that we can make genuine decisions and not merely apparent ones. Doing what we are all familiar with in taking decisions is, in fact, what we mean by making a genuine decision. Physical determinism and free will cannot, therefore, be incompatible. The importance here of our *experience* of free will suggests a connection with consciousness, as follows: a condition of acting freely is being aware of what one is doing, and awareness entails being conscious. This would make consciousness only a necessary condition and not a sufficient one — a condition without which there could be no free action, and not that which makes the action a free one. However, this is sufficient to give us a clue about how consciousness is related to moral agency, and therefore to the relevance of what comes next.

Before becoming too optimistic regarding the usefulness of the concept of consciousness, however, let us look a little at what it means to say that something is conscious, and the grounds on which we might assert this. In one respect consciousness is very easy to characterize, in another respect, very hard. On the one hand, we can make it plain what we mean by consciousness by saying, for example, that it is that feature people have when they are awake but lack when they are asleep — the feature of *awareness*. Now, some things are such that they are conscious some of the time (humans, for instance, and probably many of the animals), whereas a lot of things, we assume, are never conscious (such as trees, typewriters, and teacups). There are some borderline cases such as earthworms and sponges, though they seldom present practical problems to us. In the light of this, on which side of the divide would the most intelligent foreseeable computers fall?

On the other hand, however, something terribly obscure about consciousness destroys the neatness of this apparently simple question. When we come to ask, "What is it that makes us ascribe consciousness to one creature and not to another?", the answer is not at all obvious. Philosophers have problems about how we know even that other *people* have minds (are capable of consciousness), let alone how we know this about other sorts of creatures. We need not meet this issue head-on, since this is not an essay in the philosophy of mind, and since the philosopher's question here is largely a question about *how* we know something and not about *whether* we know it (a distinction which is often inadequately grasped by non-philosophers). On what grounds, then, do we normally conclude that another creature is conscious? It has something, certainly, to do with the fact that consciousness tends to go with being alive. Yet it cannot be simply that consciousness is to be equated with being a living thing, otherwise it would follow that plants were conscious and that no machine (in the usual sense) ever could be, neither of which seems acceptable as it stands. The living things to which we are apt to ascribe consciousness are the animals, which are animated, move, have central nervous systems, and can be said to interact with their environment. This accords quite happily with the minimum conditions discussed above. The acute philosophical problem lies in the fact that it is not clear that one can argue inductively or by analogy, in the usual sorts of ways, for or against the consciousness of a creature other than oneself. Here the basic philosophical question about other minds does begin to exert an influence. It reminds us that the only direct evidence that anyone has for consciousness is in his or her own case. If we wish to establish, say, that creatures which have hearts also have kidneys, we have enough cases of the two things going together to be in a position to generalize, but the same is not true with consciousness. Each of us has only one observed case to go on, our own self — an apparently poor basis for induction or analogy if there ever was one! On what grounds are we entitled to assert that all creatures with central nervous systems are conscious? One may point to the fact that the central nervous system has been identified as the brain plus the chief means of bringing sensory information to the brain and impulses from it; and that the brain has been identified as the major seat of the consciousness. But all this is to beg the question. There is no obvious logical contradiction in adopting the position that no other creatures except oneself are conscious at all (the solipsist position). If they are not, their brains are not the seats of their consciousness. Any possible outward behavior or response to stimuli is consistent with the hypothesis that they are not actually conscious but merely responding in a "sleep-walking" way: alive and animate, but permanently unconscious. Anyone who really believed this would be some kind of psychopath; hence the insistence above that the real question is about how and not whether we know that others are conscious. Yet it brings home the point about our lack of understanding of what it is which entitles us to say that a particular organism is conscious. The criteria according to which we habitually operate are instinctive, intuitive, and apparently based largely on the degree of likeness between ourselves and the organism in question: other people are conscious beyond doubt, most other animals are perhaps just a little more doubtful, sponges and the like are very doubtful indeed, and the consciousness of plants is only believed in by the radically eccentric. But it is very hard to justify this classification, except perhaps by pointing to the relative complexity of sensory organs. Yet we have already seen that a wedge can be driven between the concepts of sentience and consciousness, by noticing that it is possible to imagine a creature possessing sensory organs, and giving appropriate outward responses when stimulated, but without being conscious.

Where does this leave us as regards the question of machine consciousness? Two things need saying at this point. The first is that any attempt to persuade us that demonstrably conscious machines could be built is bound to fail on philosophical grounds, simply because *nothing at all* is *demonstrably* conscious. The second is that if we were to create an artifact which exhibited all the signs we normally associate with consciousness, there would be little point in calling it a machine. It would, as we have seen above, need to have sensory organs and means of manipulating the world. It would need to be alive and responsive, as well as being able to convince us by communication with us that it was capable of some genuine thinking. At this point the concepts of machine and computer simply break down. It begins to look, therefore, as though *anything which is a good candidate for being a moral agent is not going to be a suitable candidate for being a machine*, and therefore that the question "Can machines ever be moral agents?" must be answered in the negative. However, the ethical issue remains of whether we would be justified in attempting to build artifact-creatures of our own making with which we must interact morally.

10. The Variety of Remedies

The preceding chapters discussed several sources of the anxiety which is sometimes expressed by people concerning the rapid growth of computing and information technology. I have looked at the question of whether information technology in itself can be considered morally neutral, at whether computerization leads to political oppression, whether machines are particularly prone to dangerous kinds of error, and in what ways if any they contribute to the invasion of privacy and to the progressive dehumanization of the environment. I discussed the implications of data technology for the concept of ownership and related rights, and finally I have peered into what the future might hold as regards the moral relations between people and machines.

There are other topics which could have been discussed but which fall more naturally within the scope of other ethical theories and debates. For example, serious questions have been raised about the moral responsibilities of programmers for the consequences of the software which they produce; software which may, for instance, have applications in the fields of nuclear or chemical weaponry, or of espionage. This issue forms part of the ongoing concern with professional ethics as related to various professions, and with the responsibilities of employees to employers versus responsibilities to the public or to the human race as a whole. In this context it is interesting to note a recent boomerang effect concerning the use of computers in surveillance: techniques are now being used by some firms to monitor the "efficiency" of computer programmers and operators themselves, by keeping an electronic record of, for example, the number of keystrokes per minute at their terminal, the number of deletions, and so on. There is also the question of what our attitude should be to the threat of jobs being lost through the large-scale introduction of modern technology, a question which in its essentials is as old as the Industrial Revolution itself, and which has been studied already from many different angles.

Few of the problems discussed in this book can be said to be new in the sense of not having been previously discussed in the literature.

What is more, a number of solutions have already been suggested with regard to many of them. In this chapter I will discuss some of the proposed remedies. I will divide these for convenience into four categories: educational, legal, technological, and social/political.

Educational Remedies

A theme that has emerged in many parts of this discussion is the number of ways in which computerization and information technology have contributed to placing the consumer on the losing end of the officialdom-citizen relationship, or of the proprietor-customer relationship. We saw in chapter 4, for example, how non-initiates can easily be bamboozled into accepting false excuses and bogus explanations for thinly disguised human error and incompetence; and in chapter 7, how matters can often be organized to serve the convenience of programmers and operators, while appearing to the layperson to be somehow inexorably dictated by the nature of the technology.

Of course, this is not something unique about information technology: in most advanced societies those without political power or economic privilege are systematically disadvantaged in such relationships. The tendency of the new technology is simply to make this process easier. One way this has been brought about is by widening the gap between those who know and those who do not know how the channels of information work. This suggests that raising the standard of general knowledge, especially toward the bottom end of the educational spectrum, may be one effective remedy for some of these ills.

However, the lack cannot be simply identified as existing at the bottom end of the conventional educational spectrum. A mature person with a very thorough liberal education might, when it comes to making sense of the microchip world, be at just as much of a disadvantage and therefore just as exploitable as an educationally subnormal child. What is needed is a more general campaign to further the aim of computer literacy.

Yet we also saw in chapter 4 how the notion of computer literacy, understood in the usual way, does not in itself provide an effective solution for the technologically disadvantaged. While a case might be made for people having a body of general computing knowledge useful in dealing with information technology in day-to-day life, it would remain small and its usefulness be severely circumscribed. Really useful knowledge of such systems tends to be far more detailed than anything an average layperson could be expected to master; and the sort of understanding which is readily accessible to the non-specialist is frequently so superficial as to be only a semblance of understanding. The situation is even worse than this. Even a person with a fair measure of competence in computing science or related disciplines can be at almost as grave a disadvantage when dealing with some manifestation of information technology which is outside his or her own specialty. Probably the best that can be aimed at in generalized computer literacy programs is the goal of instilling into the non-expert a degree of self-confidence when dealing with situations of this kind: the sort of self-confidence which comes not from knowing all or even most of what there is to be known about a subject, but from knowing how much there is be known and what kind of thing.

There remains always the possibility that in the future changing patterns of employment in response to new technology will require that large sections of the population possess broad specialist knowledge of computing as a matter of course. There is, however, little sign of this at the moment. Until such a time as there is, educational remedies alone are likely to be of very limited effectiveness.

Legal Remedies

In the cases of threats to liberty and to personal privacy, we saw how a great deal of faith has been placed on privacy and data protection legislation as panaceas. Such legislation now exists in most technologically advanced countries and is continually spreading. A Privacy Act became law in the United States in 1974, and Britain adopted a Data Protection Bill in 1984. Similar data-protection legislation has been enacted in Austria, Denmark, France, Iceland, Luxembourg, Norway, Sweden, and elsewhere. These measures have aimed mainly at having data banks registered and monitored, and at giving members of the public the opportunity to find out what personal files exist on them in public and private data banks and to correct and update any inaccurate information.

The trouble with provisions of this kind, however, is that they will only operate successfully under conditions which they do nothing to bring about. The first and most obvious problem is that the subject of stored data may not even know that such a law exists; in countries like Britain and the United States where a significant proportion of the population is unable even to name the Prime Minister or the President, there is little hope for widespread familiarity with the details of recent legislation. The laws concerning data protection tend to be, *par excellence*, not laws which actually protect the citizen, but laws which make it possible for citizens to protect themselves — provided they possess the knowledge and the motivation to do so.

Motivation is as important as knowledge. By motivation we need not mean simply sufficient interest in looking after one's own rights to do something about it. Motivation of the appropriate kind exists where there is a general confidence in the possibility of the individual's being able to make a significant difference to anything by taking action. The evidence is that this kind of confidence is not a prominent feature of our societies.

A more practical reservation concerning data protection legislation, especially in Britain, is that its motivation is less the disinterested wish to see that individuals are protected than the necessity of conforming to international standards. Although the initial impetus internationally has undoubtedly been connected with a sincere desire to protect the citizen against breaches of privacy and unwarranted surveillance, this provides a motive for other, less libertarian legislators to fall into line superficially, owing largely to international pressure, which may otherwise adversely affect that government's chances of gaining access to, or gaining the commercial benefits from, processing the information in question. A typical expression of doubts about motives behind data-protection legislation is the following report from the British-based Campaign for the Freedom of Information:

> There was widespread concern that other countries might use their data protection laws to cut off business with British data processors. To avoid this the Council of Europe prepared a Data Protection Convention to establish minimum standards for processing personal information by computers. The British Data Protection Act is designed to meet the bare minimum standards of the Convention so that the United Kingdom can join the club. Because of this the British government has taken advantage of every possible loophole in the Convention, many of which affect the right of "subject access".[1]

A further problem regarding legal remedies lies in the fact that they are very difficult to formulate without putting the individual's privacy in jeopardy almost to the same extent as they act to protect it. Such laws tend to lead to the necessity to document all computerized records on individuals, so as to make it possible for the relevant authorities to know what information exists, where and on whom, and in what form. Once this is the case, the way is then open for such authorities to demand access to the information itself where this is judged to be somehow in the public or national interest. For example, when the British Data Protection Bill was still going through Parliament, a civil rights organization gathered the kinds of worries expressed in the following extract from the *London Times*:

> The . . . National Council for Civil Liberties, says that parts of the bill coming before MPs today would enable confidential information to be handed to the police or to tax or immigration officials even if no crime has been committed. Under one clause the user of a registered data bank may disclose information from the bank to anyone requiring it for national security, prevention or detection of crime, prosecution of offenders, or for tax purposes. . . . Anyone in charge of a medical data bank could give information on a patient to a police officer, tax inspector, or customs and excise official. Similarly, government officials could breach the confidentiality of unemployment benefit files, and banks the confidentiality of clients' accounts.[2]

Technological Remedies

It has sometimes been suggested that the solutions to problems raised by technology might themselves be technological. That is, it has been proposed that the very capabilities which give rise to moral difficulties of this kind might play a significant role in dispelling them. Take one recent example:

> The threat to privacy imposed by integrated data banks is often discussed. . . . It seems reasonable to assume that technology is something we must learn to live with and to adapt to. We are suffering radical changes which apparently can't be stopped and shouldn't be stopped anyway. . . . Technology, designed to solve problems, has created them. Can the problem-solving process be turned on itself? We have been discussing . . . the individual and the feeling of alienation which is produced by powerful forces which he does not understand. I . . . suggest that Technology can make an essential contribution to the solution.[3]

There is a serious point to this. The more practical worries, for example, those which concern data security rather than data protection, can sometimes be approached in this way. Yet the *moral* problems with which we have largely been concerned are not on the whole amenable to purely technological solutions. It is always a mistake to think that matters of social, political, and economic principle can be resolved simply by throwing more research at them. The truth is that they are usually moral questions and are a matter of intelligent deliberation and decision, rather than of discovery or invention.

It is worrying also that the point of view which sees the answer to such problems as lying in more or better technology tends to be associated with the advocacy of "technocracy." Technocracy is the doctrine that the best people to advise on the desirability of various options, to guide us, and ultimately to govern us must be the scientists or technologists. If our problems arise from scientific capabilities, who better to solve them than those who know best about such matters?

A popular argument for technocracy is as follows. Politicians are not experts in such areas as technology, and typically have little interest or specialist knowledge in technical matters at all. The public who elect (if it is a democracy) these politicians know even less. If technology is going to play the prominent role in our future which we suppose it will, ought not those responsible for these innovations play a large part in organizing that future? In other words, ought we not to leave the question of the way in which technology is going to develop to those who are best fitted to the task through dealing with it more and understanding it?

Some people have gone even farther and argued that government in general is better placed in the hands of scientists than of politicians. The objection to this line of argument ought to be obvious: unless accountability would go by the board it is difficult to see how the "experts" could avoid becoming simply a new race of politicians, with all the drawbacks of a race of professional politicians. We will concentrate on a more limited, but perhaps therefore more appealing, idea, that when it comes to the putting into practice of science and technology, the people we should turn to are the scientists and technologists. This position has been expressed, in a relatively mild form — sometimes so mild that it is hard to know what is being said — by C.P. Snow in his *Science and Government* and elsewhere.

The trouble with technocracy — the giving of a policy-making role as opposed to a merely consultative role, to experts — concerns the relations between means and ends in public life. The picture offered by adherents of technocracy tends to be that of a fixed and limited set of aims, to be achieved by pursuing whatever means turn out to be the most efficient given the purpose. In other words, according to this picture there is no real problem about what our aims should be: as in

More's *Utopia* we can assume the existence of a set of ultimate political objectives which would satisfy everybody, on which all could agree. All that remains is to discover the means of realizing them, and this, of course, is where the importance of the policy-making boffins is supposed to lie. Neat and simple as this picture may be, it embodies a hopeless confusion: it makes a sharp distinction between means and ends and it regards ends as static. Finally, while suggesting that there is no real difficulty in deciding what ends to pursue, it presents the choice of means as a question of pure expediency. So what is wrong with all this?

First, ends and means in politics are not easily separated in practice. It is tempting to think of this as a defect or confusion in our thinking. In a well-ordered society would we not have a clear political blueprint embodying a distinction between a set of agreed aims and a program of policies which appear to be the optimum means of achieving these aims? But this approach begs most of the important questions. For the idea of society as a whole having aims or goals, as though these were somehow separate from the day-to-day functioning of a community, is an odd one. It is like talking about the goal or function of an organism like a human being. The fact is, people's lives do not divide up neatly in this way; nor should they be expected to. Secondly, and following from this, it cannot be expected that the aims and aspirations of one generation will be those of another, even where they can be clearly identified. Ideals are not static but dynamic. Thirdly, to regard technological skills as the best qualification for making policy decisions is to ignore the fact that, even where we have clearly defined aims and the means to fulfil them, the question of whether to do so or not may well be a moral decision: there may be reasons, for example, to do with the cost in human suffering or inconvenience, which would or should lead us to hesitate before using the means open to us. In short, smart technology cannot replace ethics, any more than ethics can replace technology.

Social and Political Remedies

In a sense, the sorts of remedy discussed so far are easy to implement. They may not be terribly effective by themselves, but at least we possess ready-made machinery for putting them into action, and perhaps this is why they have been so often seized upon as remedies despite their overall ineffectiveness: the natural reaction of people is to do what they know how to do best, rather than what would in fact be the best thing to do. Sociopolitical remedies, by contrast, are the hardest to implement, or even to decide upon. But there is no doubt that, where appropriate, they represent a more fundamental, a more thoroughgoing approach than the kind of piecemeal solutions discussed above.

The three general conditions which have been mentioned for minimizing the potentially harmful consequences of information technology refer more to broad traits of a society than to those features which explicitly concern either information or technology. They are openness, accountability, and what I shall call cooperation. We will look at these in turn.

Openness. It has emerged in various contexts in this book that one condition of averting some of the more worrying social consequences of data technology is a greater degree of openness regarding the purposes for which such technology is used. It is a notorious fact that governments are reluctant to disclose their activities in the field of data and information. In Britain the Official Secrets Act is used to cover a large number of areas often only minimally connected with national security and the like, many of which are widely thought to be inappropriate as objects of such secrecy. Most other Western states operate similar arrangements of some sort. That there is a tension between such measures and the claim to be democratic is a point which ought not to need laboring. It is essential to the working of a democratic state that citizens should as far as possible have available the entire range of facts relevant to the purposes of collective decision-making. Otherwise, the result is a democracy in name only. If this is the case in general, it is especially so when the information is about information: that is, when the subject matter which we wish to be brought out into the open concerns the ways in which those who govern us keep their fingers on facts about the governed. There can be no place in a democracy for secrecy regarding the relationship between rulers and ruled. The principle immediately suggests itself (though it is indifferently observed in practice) that the onus is squarely on the representative of officialdom to show why secrecy is necessary in a particular sort of case, and not on the opponent to make out a case for disclosure. Yet the natural secretiveness of bureaucracy, combined with the inherent complexity of the subject matter, tends to pull in the direction of withholding rather than of disclosure.

The above refers only to public bodies. Private organizations also tend to espouse secrecy as a means of safeguarding their operations against complaint, protest, and competition. Some of the legislation mentioned here has ameliorated the situation, though often it barely serves to curb the worst excesses. It remains true that much information-gathering, processing, and use goes on regarding individuals who are totally unaware that this is happening at all. Data-protection legislation can only operate effectively against a background of publicity and openness in which citizens not only have rights, but are aware of them and can do something about them. This leads me to the next consideration.

Accountability. One reason why we require both public and private organizations to be forthcoming with details of their operations, particularly in connection with data-handling, is that we want them to be accountable. That is to say, we hope that their activities will be open to public scrutiny and control. In the case of public bodies this is relatively straightforward: for something to be a public concern it ought to be under the control of the people as a whole. Private organizations are in a somewhat different position. They might be accountable to governing bodies, to shareholders, and so on, but are by no means accountable in the same way as public bodies. In their case the best that can probably be hoped for is: (a) that standards be embodied either in law or in some other enforceable code of practice and (b) that some mechanism should exist for ensuring that a private organization cannot attain the lack of accountability which arises from having a monopoly in its particular field.

The difficulty of making private bodies truly accountable should, however, give us cause to consider the desirability of allowing them the kind of extensive rights to hold and process computerized data that publicly controled bodies have. It is true that some data-protection legislation has served to impose limits here, though the restrictions tend hardly to allay all worries. This is especially so when we consider the number of private concerns, from mail-order firms to banks to credit agencies and even more sinister bodies (some dealing with such things as individuals' political "soundness"), which keep information on us; and the difficulty of ensuring compliance even with such codes as exist. If the specter of an elected government or its agencies having the kinds of capabilities we have been talking about is alarming, surely that of a private, unelected body possessing the same sort of powers is even more so. Public bodies, at least in theory, exist to serve the interests of the people as a whole. Private organizations carry no such brief even in theory: only uncritical acceptance of some "hidden hand" theory can offer an apparent guarantee that the long-term consequences tend toward the universal benefit. This brings me to the third condition.

Cooperation. I have used this term, for want of a better one, to mean the reverse of competition or competitiveness. In chapter 7 I suggested that one reason for the alleged dehumanization of our daily environment is that the need (our society and culture being what it is) for many agencies to compete with each other, often as a condition of survival, forces certain types of decision on them *malgré eux.* That is, it doesn't matter what a particular organization would *like* to do in a given case: if a given course of action is necessary in order to be effectively competitive, then it *must* be adopted or the organization will cease to count because it will cease to exist. This applies most chiefly to private concerns, though we should not forget the extent to which even public bodies often compete with each other for funds, prestige, and the chance to expand. Even individual persons are to some extent encouraged to regard themselves as in constant competition with each other: as employees, consumers, and in many other ways. I noted earlier how the fact of A's using some technological means of saving time, for example, and thereby superficially "achieving" more in a given period puts an automatic pressure on B to do likewise. The result tends to be that everybody gets what nobody wants. Surely few people can seriously wish to spend all their time saving time, or all their effort saving labor. If we do not want our lives to be run by the very devices which are intended to make them freer, if we do not want our environment to be dehumanized by the technology which has a potential to make them more human, then we must begin by curbing the tendency to make ourselves our own worst enemies. For, by making us all into the enemies of each other, the ideal of unbridled competitiveness inevitably means just this.

I do not deny that competition has a role in business, politics, sport, or whatever. The point is that, where competitiveness is thought desirable, it must be because for some special reason it is mutually beneficial given the particular circumstances, and not because of some general commitment to competition for its own sake. To elevate universal antagonism to the status of a moral imperative, as some politicians of a certain kind have attempted to do in recent years, is to court social and ecological disaster; for it is bound to remove important decisions about the kind of world we want to live in from our own hands. The choice of whether we use the new technology to create a more congenial environment or to make a technological jungle is too important to be left to the blind forces of the marketplace.

Nature, Culture, and Technology

I have argued in this book that it is futile to talk about the ethics of information technology as though this were something distinct and isolated from the rest of our society and its purposes. It begins to look as if the considerations relevant to averting the potentially harmful consequences of the new technology are the same as those necessary for ensuring a free and fair form of social organization in general: openness, accountability, cooperation. These ideas are deeply rooted in established traditions within Western political philosophy, though they may not be as fashionable today as at certain periods of modern history.

That the real remedies should boil down in this way is, however, to be expected in the light of what was said as far back as chapter 1: *new* social values make no sense, though we may discover progressively the importance of certain values, and though new threats to our basic values may always have to be dealt with. Sometimes new responses are necessary to counter new threats. Yet in the end it would be very odd if the threads of our various collective problems did not tend to converge, did not tend to reveal an underlying pattern, a basic repertoire of ways in which things can be beneficial or harmful to the fabric of a society. I have tried to show how these worries, which superficially are about information technology, tie in with broader and more fundamental issues in ethics, in social and political philosophy, and in other areas that between them form quite a wide sweep. To ignore these relationships would be to perpetuate the mistake about which I spoke earlier in this chapter, and which was discussed before in chapter 2, of regarding the sphere of science and technology as somehow autonomous — as though we could resolve political disputes without bringing in politics, social problems without any sociology, and so on. Technology will *not* work this sort of magic, however nice that might be. The important fact about technology is that *on its own* it can solve nothing, any more than *on its own* it can create problems of the kind we have been discussing.

That was my point for talking about neutrality. The good or harm in question arises not out of the mere technical *capacity* to do this or that, but from the *propensity* to do one thing rather than another. The really interesting questions, from the moral point of view, arise when we start to ask for the explanations of these propensities: in other words, the ethics really begins where the technology leaves off. As far as these propensities are concerned, it has been suggested that their origins can be divided into those which derive from our nature purely as human creatures, and those which arise from the particular cultural background within which we operate. Thus we might wish to regard the cluster of issues we have been discussing as arising from the interplay of three factors that can be represented like this:

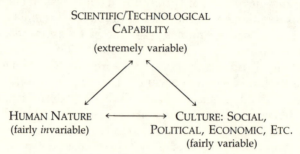

SCIENTIFIC/TECHNOLOGICAL
CAPABILITY

(extremely variable)

HUMAN NATURE ⟷ CULTURE: SOCIAL,
(fairly *in*variable)   POLITICAL, ECONOMIC, ETC.
(fairly variable)

This is crude, but there is a point to it. I distinguished in chapter 2 between two ways in which facts as such are relevant to moral deliberation: as *tools* and as *constraints*. This again is a rough but by no means arbitrary classification. Tools are what present themselves to us as enabling certain moves on our part. Prominent among these will be facts concerning the availability of particular kinds of technological capacity. Constraints, on the other hand, form the background against which we have to act. To reintroduce the analogy of a game, we may say that tools are like the bats, balls, or racquets with which we make our move, and constraints are analogous to the rules, the placement of the goalposts, the positions of the other players, and the rest of the things in the light of which we make it. One interesting thing about the three-way distinction is the ambivalent status of technology. Human nature clearly ranks as a fairly invariant factor in the calculation, while culture obviously changes, though not in a way which can be easily brought about by the effort of any given person. The state of our technology is in a peculiar position with regard to this paradigm.

I warned in chapter 2 against the danger of seeing technology solely as a set of tools available for our use in given situations but not really forming part of the background against we make our moral choices. I also pointed to the reasons — the idea of neutrality and so on — which make this dangerous picture attractive. It is now time, however, to say something about the opposite error: that of seeing technology only as a constraint. This comes about in quite a different way. For although technology is seen by most people as being essentially dynamic, always changing, always developing, it is too often assumed that somehow its development is already mapped out in advance, in such a way that we can do little or nothing to influence the forms which it is going to take or the applications and policies which it will be designed to serve. These assumptions are as widespread as they are inimical to our thesis here, and it will be appropriate to end by saying a little, positive as well as negative, on this topic.

Which Way Is Forward?

We have seen a great deal in this book about such notions as advances and progress. To return briefly to the distinction made in chapter 2 between the acquisition of new *facts* and the acquisition of new *things*, it is safe to say that the accumulation of knowledge, considered simply as such, always represents an advance of a sort, even if it turns out to serve more as a warning than as a positive help. However, the accumulation of technology in the sense of ever newer and more original artifacts carries no such guarantee. Yet all too often we encounter the uncritical assumption that every innovation of a technical sort represents an advance in some wider sense; that all change is by definition progress.

What underlies such an attitude is clearly a belief in what we may term technological determinism. This is the (often unarticulated) view that the development of technology follows laws of its own logic, dragging in its wake the rest of human life and culture. While most forms of determinism are in various ways implausible, this form has probably less to be said for it than most. The problem with all such determinisms is their onesidedness. It is hard to believe that economic forces, or social structures, or individual psychology, or genetics, or climate is the one factor which gives the whole story. In the case of technology it is especially difficult to accept that the influence is entirely in one direction, from technology to the other aspects of life. Although this is often insufficiently recognized, this is the necessary belief for supposing that human interests independent of technology do not affect *its* development at least least as much as it affects them. It ought to be obvious that the course of past and future technology depends on a whole range of interests and motives, which induce researchers to turn their attention in this or that direction, to become interested in one line of development rather than another — interests and motives which need not themselves be the result of any influence from trends in technology.

The direction of technological change is, then, *up to us*. There is no invisible track, predetermined and stretching into the future, marked "progress." This is not to say that progress does not occur, much less to suggest that one direction is as good as any other. It is only to make the point that the decision regarding which course represents a real benefit for the human race, in other words, which direction is to be regarded as forward, is our decision, for which we, and not some abstract force such as progress, are responsible.

Sometimes, technological determinism of this sort *is* bound up with some other kind of determinism. It may, for example, be thought that our apparent lack of control over technological development comes from a lack of control over our social environment in general. Yet I have argued that it is precisely by planning, by taking conscious decisions about the kind of society in which we want to live, that we can begin to control the effects which modern technology, and information technology in particular, will have on our lives. It has been argued that we must look to the wider social environment if we wish to find effective and lasting remedies to the problems we have been addressing. We may, of course, identify these problems in the first instance by studying the detailed effects of the technology as such, but, having done so, to fail to put them in the broader context is to risk treating the symptoms and not the disease.

The case is often worse than this. If we begin from specific and isolated problems which are summed up in a heading such as "social effects of computerization," it is apt to appear, as we saw above, that no cure is possible; as though technological change has a life of its own and runs on inexorably in one single direction; as though there is an unstoppable force called progress, whose price is to accept whatever form it takes, whatever its concomitants.

The Information Game

This brings us to the question which was left hanging at the end of the Introduction, of the seemingly irreverent title of this book. By referring to the sort of activity the ethics of which have been discussed above as a game, it is not intended to suggest that such activities are trivial, negligible, or necessarily divorced from the central business of our lives. Games, in the most literal sense, are capable of being the reverse of all these things. It is rather to make a point about human choice. If anything is characteristic of games (and certain devotees of Wittgenstein will no doubt feel obliged to insist that nothing is), it is surely that we can choose whether or not to take part in them. Even if game-playing in general is a natural and ubiquitous form of human activity, the choice of which games we play is ours. When we do take part in games the rules are also up to us. This is not, of course, to say that any individual can walk onto the field and alter the rules at will, but that rules can be made and changed by a consensus of all interested parties. In this way games are unlike those activities which involve us in seeking the bare necessities of our lives, which we might call compulsory activities, whose rules are dictated by the constraints of our environment. True, information technology may, in certain circumstances, be closely connected with the business of making a living. Clearly, however, it has more to do with the nature and quality of our lives than with the mere preservation and sustenance of them. Few decisions regarding how such technology should be used are going to be unavoidable, life-or-death decisions: that is, they will not be of this kind unless *we* intentionally or unintentionally bring it about that they are.

It must be admitted that the implicit distinction between compulsory and non-compulsory activities is debatable. What counts as a survival-level activity in one environment or culture might not in another, and vice versa. It ought, however, to be fairly clear that some human concerns are farther removed from the bedrock of sheer natural necessity than others. In general the more distant an activity is from this bedrock, the more choice we have regarding whether and how we engage in it. As will now be obvious, one of my concerns is to locate most manifestations of information technology pretty far away from the bedrock, well within the area where human choice has much free play. This is, of course, a huge generalization. There are many ways in which individual lives and livelihoods may depend upon such technology, and to that extent it is a survival activity from the point of view of those involved (fighter pilots, patients on computer-controlled medication, and so on). But for mankind as a whole it is not, however much it may contribute to human well-being or the reverse.

As I have said, the purpose here is not to devalue the role of information technology for good or harm. It is probably one of the greatest achievements of the "developed" societies that over the last few centuries they have dramatically expanded these areas of free choice in human life. This is not an observation regarding political doctrine, or at least not explicitly so. It is meant rather as a comment on the effects of technology on the lives of the mass of people living. It will, however, be clear already that I wish to argue for the practical inseparability of scientific, technological, economic, and political policies — and therefore of the questions of what is to count as an advance, a stagnation or a retrogression in any of these areas. Life does not come neatly compartmentalized.

Our freedom to indulge in games — even the most serious of them — is hard-won. Technology, including information technology, has itself played a role in making it possible, and this is one of the most persuasive things which can be said in its behalf. To make something possible is not, however, to make it come about: it requires also the will and the resources. Herein lies the danger of accepting too readily the idea that not only change, but the very direction of change, is inevitable. This is to allow the games to take over, and to let the vehicles of our freedom become the instruments of our own slavery.

Two of the themes running through this book have been the influence of the human factor — those motives and inclinations which are fairly constant in human nature — and of the cultural factor — the assemblage of concepts, presuppositions, and prejudices that overlay our thinking and depend on time and place. What must be finally emphasized is that neither of these factors is totally beyond our control. To reason from the premise that both are eternally with us in some form or other, as a rigid intellectual straightjacket, is to embrace a principle which is belied by the very existence of social change or development of any sort. In particular it is a feature of such cultural or even more deep-rooted presuppositions that once they are recognized as such, the situation has already altered to allow for their conscious modification; and to deny that they can ever be identified would be a very contentious claim indeed, requiring much further argument in its support.

But this is not meant to be an essay in the philosophy or sociology of knowledge or value as such. The importance of this strand has been chiefly in its bearing on the question of what responses can be thought reasonable and realistic in the face of social and technological trends over which we as individuals, and perhaps even collectively, appear to have little control. If one thing above all has emerged, it might be the following. It is not merely compliance or participation in human activities which shapes the world, either for better or worse, but also reflection on them. Reflection makes the difference between simply swimming with the tide of our own particular epoch and being instrumental in shaping the next. We now have at our disposal an enormous and growing armory of technological know-how. But knowing *how* is not enough; it is knowing what, whether, and above all *why* that gives us collectively a measure of control over our way of life — that allows us to master the constraints of brute necessity and gives rise to genuine choice. To revert more specifically to our topic, it is not a shortage of information or of ways of processing it which constitutes the real problem in our future: it is the need for a well-thought-out rationale of what we want the information *for*, and why. In other words, it is reflection on values, not just on facts and their acquisition, that is the most serious lack.

Is philosophy also then a game as understood above? Certainly it is not a survival activity in the narrow sense. Yet it is through philosophy that reflection on values is able to take place, allowing us to consider the relation between where we stand at a given time and where it appears on reflection that we *ought* to be. It is part of a fully human life that it should be thus questioned. If philosophy is a game, therefore, it is by far the most serious of games. Philosophers and technologists, or any other group of practitioners whose practice affects our lives, ignore each other at their peril — and that of us all.

Notes

Introduction

1. *A National Survey of the Public's Attitudes Toward Computers* (*Time* Magazine, with the American Federation of Information Processing Societies, 1987).
2. See, e.g., Robert M. Baer *The Digital Villain* (New York: Addison Wesley, 1972).

Chapter 1. New Problems for Old

1. Friedrich Nietzsche *Thus Spake Zarathustra* (1883–92), *Beyond Good and Evil* (1886).
2. B.F. Skinner *Beyond Freedom and Dignity* (London: Cape, 1972).
3. For a discussion of the concept of common knowledge, see Jane Heal "Common Knowledge" *Philosophical Quarterly* 28 (April 1978): 116–31.
4. The combination of computers and telecommunications networks is sometimes known as "telematics."
5. C.J. Date *An Introduction to Database Systems* 4th ed. (New York: Addison Wesley, 1986) Vol. 1 p. 5.
6. D. Burnham *The Rise of the Computer State* (New York: Random House, 1983) p. 81.

Chapter 2. Technology as Morally Neutral

1. Peter Medawar *Pluto's Republic* (Oxford: Oxford University Press, 1982) p. 35.
2. William James *Pragmatism* (1907) and *The Meaning of Truth* (1909).
3. C.S. Peirce *Collected Papers* ed. Harteshorne et al. (Cambridge Mass.: Harvard University Press, 1931–58), Vol. 5 and Vol. 8.
4. John Dewey "The Development of American Pragmatism" in his *Philosophy and Civilization* (Cambridge Mass.: Harvard University Press, 1931) Ch. 2.
5. A correspondence theory of truth is, roughly speaking, a theory according to which something is true (if it is true) in virtue of a "correspondence" between it and the facts, or between it and some features of the world. Such theories are usually contrasted with pragmatist, and with coherence theories of truth.
6. On the topic of scientific realism see, e.g., Rom Harré *The Philosophies of Science* 2nd ed. (Oxford: Oxford University Press, 1984).
7. A.J.P. Taylor *The First World War: An Illustrated History* (Harmondsworth: Penguin Books, 1981) p. 20.

Chapter 3. Is Big Brother Watching?

1. G.L. Simons *Privacy in the Computer Age* (Manchester: National Computing Centre, 1982) pp. 43–4.

2. Hannah Arendt *The Origins of Totalitarianism* (New York: Jovanovich, rev. ed. 1973) pp. 323–4.
3. Aristotle *Politics*, Book 1, Ch. 2, trans. T.A. Sinclair (Penguin Books, 1962) p. 28.
4. Saint Augustine *City of God* trans. Henry Bettenson, ed. David Knowles (Penguin Books, 1972) p. 599.
5. Robert Nozick *Anarchy, State and Utopia* (Oxford: Blackwell, 1974) p. 12.
6. Proudhon *The General idea of the Revolution in the Nineteenth Century* trans. J.B. Robinson (London: Freedom Press, 1923) pp. 293–4, modified (quoted by Nozick in *Anarchy, State and Utopia*).
7. Henry David Thoreau *Civil Disobedience* (1849).

Chapter 4. To Err Is Human

1. For other good examples, see Simons *Privacy in the Computer Age*.
2. On this topic see, e.g., S.R. Gring "Introducing Computer Literacy" *Educational Leadership* 40 (Oct. 1982) p. 69; also J.E. Inskeep Jr. "Computer Literacy: What It Is and Why We Need It" *Curriculum Review* 21 (May 1981) pp. 138–41.

Chapter 5. Private Lives

1. William L. Prosser "Privacy" *California Law Review*" 48 pp. 383–423.
2. Sissela Bok *Secrets* (Oxford: Oxford University Press, 1984) p. 11.
3. M. Warner and M. Stone *The Data Bank Society* (London: Allen and Unwin, 1970) pp. 125–6.
4. Report of the Committee on Data Privacy, Chairman Sir Norman Lindop, Command 7341 (HMSO, 1978) para. 2.04.
5. Edward J. Bloustein "Privacy as an Aspect of Dignity" *New York University Law Review* 39 (1964) 962–1007.
6. Stafford Beer in *Computing Weekly* 21st August 1969 (quoted by Warner and Stone in *The Data Bank Society*).

Chapter 6. More about Privacy

1. C.C. Gotlieb and A. Borodin *Social Issues in Computing* (New York: Academic Press, 1973) p. 75.
2. Simon Kinnersley in *The Daily Mail* 17th December 1982.
3. *Times Higher Education Supplement* 2nd December 1983.
4. John Stuart Mill *Utilitarianism* (1863).
5. See R.M. Hare *Moral Thinking* (Oxford: Oxford University Press, 1981).

Chapter 7. The Non-Human Face of Technology

1. C. Northcote Parkinson *Parkinson's Law, or the Pursuit of Progress* (London: John Murray, 1958) p. 11.
2. Joseph Weizenbaum *Computer Power and Human Reason* (San Francisco: Freeman, 1977).

3. James A. Moor "Are There Decisions Computers Should Never Make?" in Deborah Johnson and John Snapper (eds.) *Ethical Issues in the Use of Computers* (Belmont, California: Wadsworth, 1985).

Chapter 8. *Ownership, Rights, and Information*

1. In practice a program would be made to terminate as soon as a square root is found, but for simplicity this feature has been omitted in the examples given.
2. On the law in this area see Colin Tapper *Computers and the Law* (London: Weidenfeld and Nicholson, 1973) and *Computer Law* (London: Longman, 1978).
3. Lord Denning, quoted in Tapper *Computer Law*.
4. Mr Justice Holmes in *Du Pont vs. Masland* (1917), quoted in Tapper *Computer Law*.
5. Thus the new *Encyclopaedia Britannica* (15th ed., 1974) Vol. 15, p. 46. "The word property is frequently used indiscriminately to denote not only objects of rights that have a pecuniary content, but also rights that persons have with respect to things. Thus, lands and chattels are said to be property, and rights, such as ownership, life estates, and easements, are likewise said to be property. Accurate legal terminology, however, usually reserves the use of the word property for the designation of rights that persons have with respect to things."
6. See R.B. Schlatter *Private Property: The History of an Idea* (New Brunswick, N.J.: Rutgers University Press, 1951, reprinted Russell and Russell, 1973).
7. See James A. Grunebaum *Private Ownership* (New York: Methuen, 1987).

Chapter 9. *Moral Attitudes to Machines?*

1. Michael Frayn *The Tin Men* (Glasgow: Collins, 1965) p. 20.
2. David Hume *A Treatise of Human Nature* (1739–40), Book 2, Part 3, Sect. 3.
3. Ibid. Book 3, Part 1, Sect. 1.
4. Immanuel Kant *Groundwork of the Metaphysics of Morals* (1785).
5. Daniel Dennett "Why You Can't Make a Computer That Feels Pain" in his *Brain Storms: Philosophical Essays on Mind and Psychology* (Hassocks: Harvester, 1978).
6. On connectionist architecture see, e.g., D.E. Rummelhart and James L. McLelland *Parallel Distributed Processing* (Cambridge: MIT Press, 1987).
7. Christopher Evans *The Mighty Micro* (London, Gollancz, 1979) p. 237.

Chapter 10. *The Variety of Remedies*

1. James Michael in *Secrets* 3 (1984).
2. *The Times* 5th April 1984 p. 4.
3. Ronald Anderton "Technological Change: The Impact of Large Technical Systems, *Technology Today*, ed. Edward de Bono (London: RKP, 1971).

Bibliography

Baer R.M. *The Digital Villain* New York: Addison Wesley, 1972.

Barnes J.A. *Who Should Know What?* Harmondsworth: Penguin Books, 1979.

Bates, Alan "Privacy: A Useful Concept?" *Social Forces* 42 (1964): 429.

Bergamini, David "Government by Computers?" *Reporter* 17th August 1961: 21.

Berger M. et al. *Freedom and Control in Modern Society* New York, 1964.

Berle A.A. Jr. "The Protection of Privacy" *Political Science Quarterly* 79 (1964): 162–8.

Bessant J.R. et al. *The Impact of Microelectronics: A Review of the Literature* London: Pinter, 1981.

Bloustein E.J. "Privacy as an Aspect of Dignity" *New York University Law Review* 39 (1964): 962–1007.

Bok, Sissela. *Secrets* Oxford: Oxford University Press, 1984.

Brenton, Myron *The Privacy Invaders* New York: Coward-McCann, 1964.

Burnham D. *The Rise of the Computer State* New York: Random House, 1983.

Burton R.P. "Transitional Data Flows: International Status, Impact and Accommodation" *Data Management* June 1980: 27–33.

Carroll J.M. *Secrets of Electronic Espionage* New York: Dutton, 1966.

Clarke A.C. "The World of the Communications Satellite" *Astronautics and Aeronautics* Feb. 1964: 45–7.

Coffey M. "US Takes a Dim View of European Data Laws" *Computing* 8th October 1981.

Committee of Ministers, Council of Europe *Convention for the Protection of Individuals with Regard to Automatic Processing of Personal Data* (Strasbourg, 18th Oct. 1980).

Connor S. "The Police Intelligence Database Is Put on Trial" *Computing* 18th Feb. 1982. "How Your Record Starts Growing Up From Birth" *Computing* 22nd April 1982: 22–3.

Cook F.J. *The FBI Nobody Knows* New York: Pyramid, 1964.

Council of Ministers, Organization for Economic Co-operation and Development OECD *Guidelines Governing the Protection of Privacy and Transborder Flows of Personal Data* 23rd Sept. 1980.

Cross, Harold *The People's Right to Know: Legal Access to Public Records and Proceedings* New York: Columbia University Press, 1953.

Dash, Samuel *The Eavesdroppers* New York: Rutgers University Press, 1959.

Date C.J. *An Introduction to Database Systems* 4th ed. New York: Addison Wesley, 1986 2 vols.

Deloitte, Haskins and Sells and the National Computing Center *The External Auditor as Privacy Inspector* NCC 1982.

Dunn E.S. "The Idea of a National Data Center and the Issue of Personal Privacy" *American Statistician* 21(1) 1967: 21–7.

Evans, Christopher *The Mighty Micro* London: Gollancz, 1979.

Ewing, Ann "Lie Detection at a Distance" *Science News Letter* 88 14th August 1965: 106.

Gassman H.P. "Privacy Implications of Transborder Data Flows: Outlook for the 1980's" in *Computers And Privacy in the Next Decade* (New York: Academic Press, 1980).

Gotlieb C.C. and Borodin A. *Social Issues in Computing* New York: Academic Press, 1973.

Gouldner A.W. and Peterson R.A. *Notes on Technology and the Moral Order* Indianapolis: Bobbs-Merrill, 1962.

Gring S.R. "Introducing Computer Literacy" *Educational Leadership* 40 (Oct. 1982): 69.

Gross M.L. *The Brain Watchers* New York, 1972.

Guidebook to the Freedom of Information and Privacy Acts New York: Clark Boardman, 1980.

Hallahans S. and May M. "The Business of Privacy" *Computerworld UK* 11th Feb. 1981: 20–21.

Heckscher, August "The Invasion of Privacy: The Reshaping of Privacy" *American Scholar* 28 (1959): 13.

Hewitt, Patricia *Privacy: The Information Gatherers* Manchester: National Computing Centre, 1977.

Hofstader S.H. and Horowitz, George *The Right of Privacy* New York, 1964.

Hunt, Roger and Shelly, John *Computers and Commonsense* 3rd ed. London: Prentice Hall, 1983.

Huxley, Aldous *Brave New World Revisited* New York: Harper, 1958.

Inskeep J.E. Jr. "Computer Literacy: What It Is and Why We Need It" *Curriculum Review* 21 (May 1981): 138–41.

Johnson, Deborah G. *Computer Ethics* Englewood Cliffs: Prentice-Hall, 1985.

——and Snapper, John W. (eds.) *Ethical Issues in the Use of Computers* Belmont, California: Wadsworth, 1985.

Kling R. "Computer Abuse and Computer Crime as Organizational Activities" *Information Privacy* Sept. 1981: 186–95.

Lamb J. "Are Forbidden Files as Secure as They Ought to Be?" *Computer Talk* 29th March 1982.

Lansdown J. "Ethics of Computer Use" *Information Privacy* Sept. 1981: 178–9.

Lasswell H.D. "The Threat to Privacy" In R.M. McIver (ed.) *The Conflict of Loyalties* New York: Harper, 1952.

Laver, Murray *An Introduction to the Uses of Computers* Cambridge: Cambridge University Press, 1976.

Lear, John "Whither Personal Privacy?" *Saturday Review* 23rd July 1966: 36.

Lobel J. "Public Good Versus Public Harm Potential of Computers" *Information Age* April 1982: 75–8.

Madgwick D. and Smythe T. *The Invasion of Privacy* London: Pitman, 1974.

Martin J.T. and Norman A.R.D. *The Computerized Society: An Appraisal of the Impact of Computers on Society over the Next 15 Years* Harmondsworth: Penguin Books, 1973.

McLauchlan W. "Privacy and Criminal Justice" *Information Privacy* March 1981: 43–9.

Millar A.R. *The Assault on Privacy: Computers, Data Banks and Dossiers* Michigan: University of Michigan Press, 1971.

Montagu, Ashley and Snyder S.S. *Man and the Computer* Wallington: Auerbach, 1972.

Mumford E. and Sackman H. *Human Choice and Computers* Amsterdam: North Holland, 1975.

National Council for Civil Liberties Publications, London, *Consuming Secrets.*

Packard, Vance *The Naked Society* New York: McKay, 1964.

Pennock J.R. and Chapman J.W. (eds.) Privacy *NOMOS* 13 (New York: Atherton Press, 1971).

Pipe G.R. "At Sea over Private Data Banks" *New Scientist* 73 (1977): 86–7.

Prosser W. "Privacy" *Columbia Law Review* 1960: 383.

Rowe R.C. *Privacy, Computers and You* Manchester: National Computing Centre, 1972.

Rule J.B. *Private Lives and Public Surveillance: Social Controls in the Computer Age* New York: Schocken, 1974.

Sackman H. and Nie N.H. *The Information Utility and Social Choice* New Jersey: AFIPS Press, 1970.

Sauverin P.T. "Privacy: the Commonsense Application of Authority" *Information Privacy* Nov. 1979: 322–5.

Schlatter R.B. *Private Property: The History of an Idea* New Brunswick, N.J., Rutgers University Press, 1951, reprinted Russell and Russell, 1973.

Shallis, Michael *The Silicon Idol* Oxford: Oxford University Press, 1984.

Shils E.A. "Privacy and Power" in Pool ed. *Contemporary Political Science: Towards Empirical Theory* New York: McGraw-Hill, 1967.

Sieghart, Paul *Privacy and Computers* London: Latimer New Dimensions, 1976.

Simons G.L. *Privacy in the Computer Age* Manchester: National Computing Centre, 1982.

Simons, Geoff *Are Computers Alive?* Hassocks: Harvester, 1983.

Tapper, Colin *Computers and the Law* London, Weidenfeld and Nicholson, 1973.

——*Computer Law* 3rd ed. London: Longman, 1978.

Taviss, Irene *The Computer Impact* New Jersey: Prentice-Hall, 1970.

Time Magazine, with the American Federation of Data Processing Organizations Inc. *A National Survey of the Public's Attitudes Toward Computers*, 1987.

Warner M. and Stone M. *The Data Bank Society: Organizations, Computers and Social Freedom* London: Allen and Unwin, 1970.

Westin, Alan F. *Privacy and Freedom* London: Bodley Head, 1967.

——and Baker M. *Databanks in a Free Society: Computers, Record Keeping and Privacy* New York: Quadrangle, 1972.

Wright J. "Safeguarding the Individual" *Computing* 4th March 1982: 28.

Yang T.L. "Privacy in English and American Law" *International and Comparative Law Quarterly* Jan. 1966.

Index

Accountability, 60–2, 65–6, 143
Algorithm, 108–11
Anderton, Roland, 155
Anonymity, 71–2
Antirealism, scientific, 28
Aquinas, St. Thomas, 47
Arendt, Hannah, 154
Aristotle, 47–8, 154
Artificial Intelligence, 124–30
Augustine of Hippo, Saint, 47–50, 154
Augustinian view of the state, 47–52
Authoritarianism, 53–5

Bacon, Francis, 24–5
Baer, Robert M., 153
Beer, Stafford, 154
Bentham, Jeremy, 48
Bloustein, Edward J, 74, 78, 154
Bok, Sissela, 154
Borodin, A., 154
Bosanquet, Benard, 47
Burnham, D., 153

Centralization, 44–5
Civil Liberties, National council for, 139
Common knowledge, 4–5
Competitiveness, 144
Computer:
    and language, 8, 125–6;
    as decision-maker, 100–3;
    as moral agent, 101–4, 121–34;
    error and, 57–66;
    learning, 130;
    memory, 9, 11, 15;
    parallelism in, 129;
    structure of, 8–10
Computer Literacy, 37–8, 62–5

Connectionism, 128–30, 155
Consciousness, 132–4
Consequentialism, 91–4
Contraception, 3
Cooperation (as opposite of competition), 144
Copyright, law of, 113–4
Crippen, Dr H.H., 83
Culture, influence of, 34–5, 145–6

Data Protection:
    legislation for, 137–9;
    recommendations on, 73
Databases, 10–13;
    interrogating, 12;
    notation for, 11–12;
    relational, 12
Date, C.J., 153
Dawson, Dr. John, 87
Dehumanization, 7, 14
Democracy, vii, 52, 142
Dennett, Daniel, 127, 155
Denning, Lord, 155
Determinism:
    physical, 131–2;
    technological, 146–8
Dewey, John, 27, 153
Dictatorship, 41–2, 44–5
Distributed representation, 129–30
Du Pont vs. Masland (1917), 155

Education, 6, 136–7
Empiricism, 28
Engels, Friedrich, 51
Ethics, professional, 135
Evans, Christopher, 155

Facts, in relation to values, 21–4
Fortress, myth of, 49–50, 51–2
Frayn, Michael, 121, 155

Freedom, see Liberty
Freedom of Information, Campaign
   for, 138
Free Will, 124, 131–2

Game, concept of, 148–51
Gotlieb, C.C., 154
Green, T.H., 47
Gring, S.R., 154
Grotius, Hugo, 47
Grunebaum, James A., 155

Hare, R.M., 92–3, 154
Harré, Rom, 153
Heal, Jane, 153
Hegel, G.W.F., 47
Hobbes, Thomas, 48
Holmes, Mr. Justice, 155
Hooker, Richard, 48
Human nature, 33, 145–6
Hume, David, 124, 155

Industrial Revolution, 33, 135
Information Technology, users of,
   6–7, 86–7, 89
Information:
   control over, 73–4, 105;
   demographic form of, 16;
   dossier form of, 16;
   gathering of, 13–14;
   privacy and, 67–8;
   processing of, 15–17;
   retrieval of, 17–19;
   storage of, 14–15;
   use of, 19
Inskeep, J.E. Jrn., 154

James, William, 27, 153

Kant, Immanuel, 119, 124, 155
Kinnersley, Simon, 154

Law, relating to computers, 111–5,
   117, 137–9
Liberty, viii, 52

Lindop Committee on Data
   Protection, 73, 154
Locke, John, 48, 119
Luther, Martin, 48

Machiavelli, Nicolo, 48
McLelland, James L, 155
Marsilius of Padua, 48
Marx, Karl, 48, 51
Medawar, Peter, 25–5, 153
Michael, James, 155
Mill, J.S., 91, 154
Montesquieu, C.L., 47
Moore, James A., 102, 155
Moral problems, nature of, 2–4
More, Thomas, 141
Morris, William, 33

Nature, State of, 50
Neutrality, moral, 21–35, 89–91
Nietzsche, F., 2, 21, 153
Norms, moral, 3
Nozick, Robert, 48, 49–50, 119, 154

Official Secrets Act, 142
Oligarchy, 42–3, 44–5
Openness, in politics, 142–34
Operationalism, 28
Orwell, George, 37, 54, 96
Other minds, Problems of, 133–4
Ownership, 105–20

Pain, 127
Paine, Tom, 48
Parkinson, C. Northcote, 96–7, 154
Patent, law of, 114–5
Philosophy, importance of, viii, 151
Pierce, C.S., 27, 153
Plato, 131
Politics:
   and solution of moral problems,
      141–4;
   in database creation, 11
Prison, Myth of, 50–2
Privacy, viii, 67–94
Prosser, W., 68–9, 154

Proudhon, Pierre Joseph, 48, 50–1, 154
Public opinion, vii
Public services, 7

Realism, scientific, 28
Rights, 67, 83, 105–20
Roles, social, 75–9
Rummelhart, D.E., 155

Schlatter, R.B., 155
Science:
as a body of knowledge, 30;
as an activity, 30;
technology and, 24–6
Secrecy, 70–1
Security forces, 7
Sentience, 126–7
Short Circuit Effect, 77, 81–5
Simons, G.L., 153
Skinner, B.F., 2, 21, 153
Snow, C.P., 140
Social Contract, 48
Software, ownership of, 107–15
Spinoza, Benedict, 48
Stone, M., 154

Tapper, Colin, 155
Taylor, A.J.P., 31, 153
Technocracy, 140
Technology:
as a remedy, 139–41;
relation to science, 24–6
Telecommunications, 9
Telematics, 153
Thoreau, Henry David, 51, 154
Totalitarianism, 40–6, 52
Trade Secrets, law of, 111–3
Truth, nature of, 26–9

Universalizability (of moral
principles), 3
Urbanization, 5
Utilitarianism, 91

Values, 2–3

Warner, M., 154
Weizenbaum, Joseph, 101–3, 154
Wittgenstein, Ludwig, 148

Younger Report on Privacy, 73